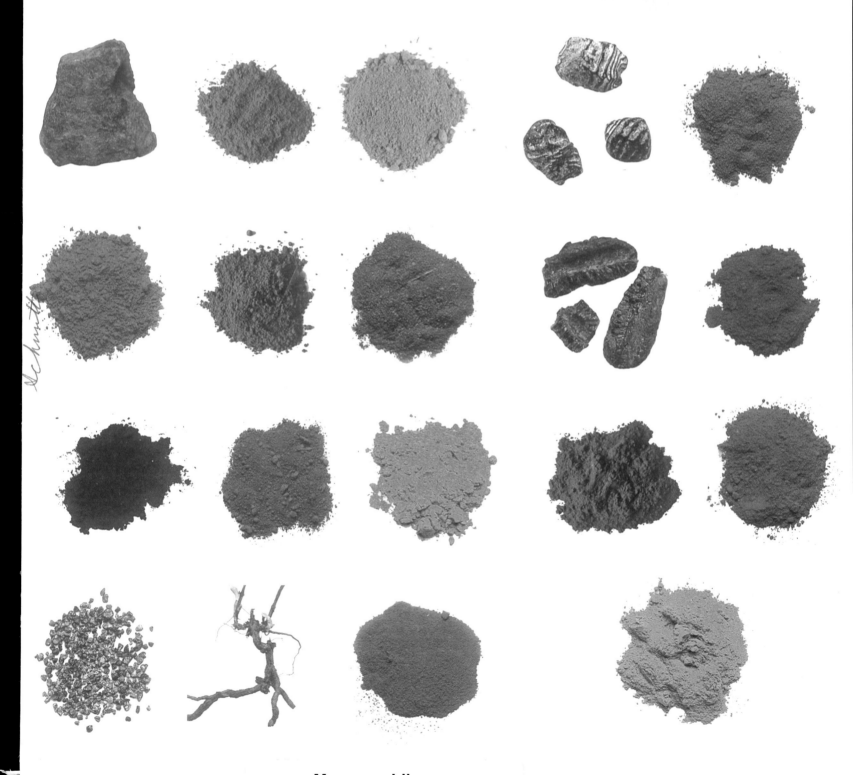

BENEATH THE SURFACE

The making of paintings

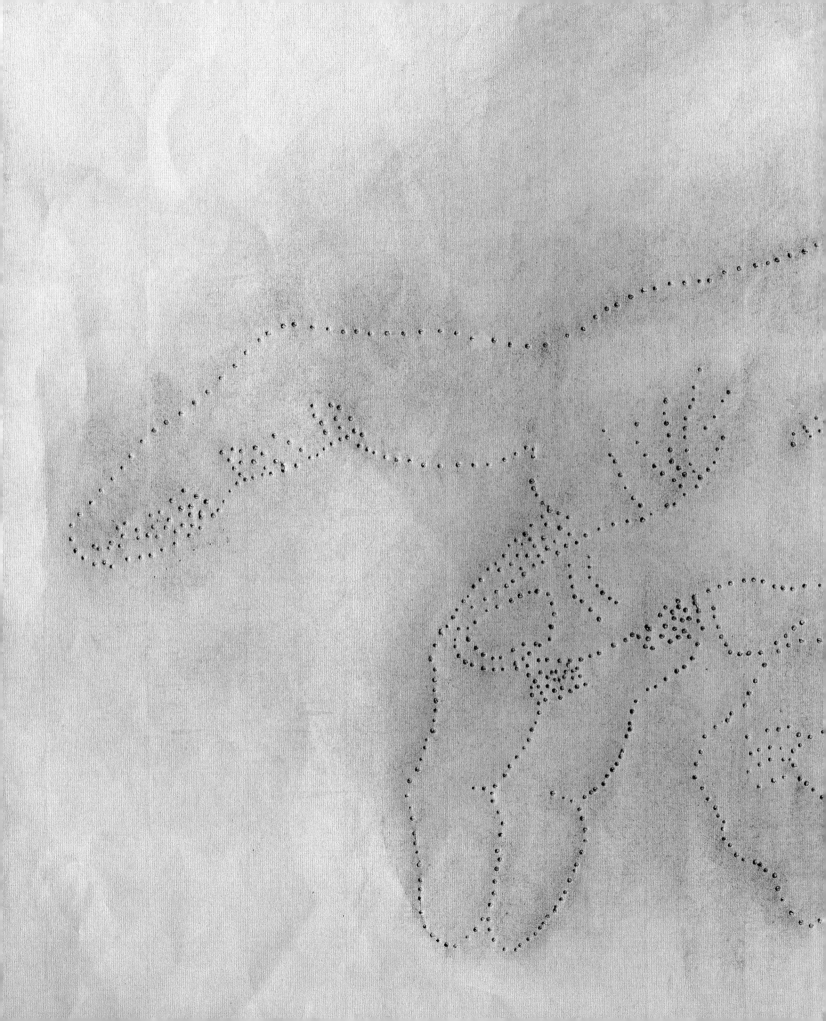

Philippa Abrahams

BENEATH THE SURFACE

The making of paintings

F

FRANCES LINCOLN LIMITED

PUBLISHERS

Frances Lincoln Limited
4 Torriano Mews
Torriano Avenue
London NW5 2RZ
www.franceslincoln.com

British Library Cataloguing in Publication Data
A catalogue record for this book is available
from the British Library.

ISBN 978-0-7112-2756-9

Printed in China

9 8 7 6 5 4 3 2 1

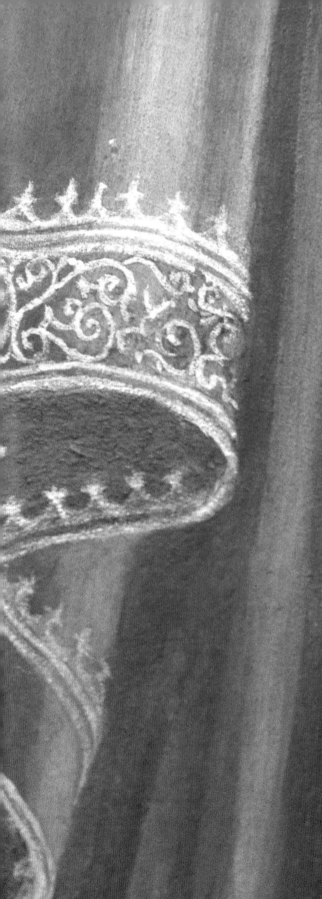

Contents

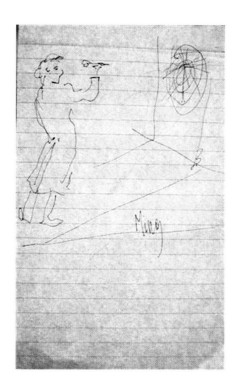

For my husband, Michael Trott, whose one
known drawing appears here

Foreword

When the Sistine Chapel underwent a major restoration in the 1980s, I was fortunate enough to be sent there for a BBC programme. The lift transporting everyone from the chapel floor to the vaults had broken down, so I had to fight vertigo and clamber up a series of ancient ladders. But once I reached the summit, Michelangelo's ceiling was near enough for me to touch. Its restorers were working on the dynamic painting where an astonished Adam is being created by the outstretched finger of a whirling, windblown God. Viewed close to, the energy and boldness of the brushmarks were breathtaking. I was astonished to discover the prodigious freedom and dash in Michelangelo's handling. Summary rather than hasty, and never skating over the many passages which needed to be thoroughly wrought, his brushwork was often applied with infectious gusto.

At one point in her immensely stimulating book, Philippa Abrahams writes: 'I am no Michelangelo.' But while reading these pages, and marvelling at her ability to offer such a wealth of first-hand insights, I am reminded of my revelatory encounter with the Sistine ceiling. Time and again she prompts me to think about art with the freshness and intensity I experienced directly underneath those vaults. Whether her subject is drawing, fresco, oil painting, egg tempera, miniatures, watercolours, acrylics or one of the many other possibilities open to exploration, Abrahams makes me imagine that I am an artist, right there in the studio or the chapel, deciding on the best way to take work in progress through to a successful conclusion.

The Sistine restoration has long since been completed, so I will never be able to reach up and touch those frescoes again. But now this invaluable book helps me appreciate, in so many distinctive and immediate ways, how artists approach the fundamental act of making.

Richard Cork
London, July 2008

Introduction

Confronted with a gloriously colourful work by Titian or one of Rembrandt's sombre portraits, we look upon a surface that has an interesting story underneath. This book takes the reader on a journey to understand how the work was made. It asks – and attempts to answer – the question, 'How was that done?' Along the way we will find out about the complexities, dangers, successes and failures of the artist's search for brilliant colours, durable tools and sensible techniques.

Artists of the past were practical people: they needed the ability to design and make a work, but they also needed to know where materials came from and how to use them, employing a complex range of techniques. It is unlikely that one particular artist had a eureka moment when he thought painting with oil might be better than egg, or that a dribble of garlic juice on a copper plate might stop the paint from sliding off. Changes in how artists worked evolved, knowledge was disseminated through artists travelling and the exchange of ideas. These ideas were not always willingly shared, recipes not always strictly accurate. It is rumoured that Rubens' workshop was one of the first to thin oil paint with turpentine and that this was supposed to be kept secret. It is also useful to remember that an artist may say one thing and do another.

The evidence of how artists worked remains in the paintings and drawings that have survived. Conservation scientists can investigate and give us more information through various kinds of analysis, including x-ray, infra-red and a battery of invasive and non-invasive tests. This book is complementary to that science and I hope enlightens in an accessible way.

We shall follow the development of Western painting and drawing techniques and materials from the natural pigments and parchment of medieval manuscripts to the cotton canvas and acrylic paints used by twentieth-century artists. Artistic practice has been punctuated by landmarks in the shape of new materials and techniques that enabled artists to work in different ways. Artists' ideas and their successful execution were dependent on materials that were acquired from near and far at vast expense or none; some of them were hazardous, and in using them artists took risks for the sake of their work.

In this book I refer to various treatises, some of them anonymous. Most frequently I quote those of Cennino Cennini (active at the end of the fourteenth century), Giorgio Vasari (1511–1574) and Francisco Pacheco (1564–1654). Each wrote about the practice of being an artist and their writings are a major source of information about how artists of the past worked and attitudes toward the profession. I recommend reading their works: their instructions for using different materials and techniques may still be followed successfully, as can some of their advice on how to conduct your life.

My favourite is *Il Libro dell' Arte* by Cennino Cennini. After over thirty years of reading this brief book, written in the late fourteenth century, every time I pick it up I still find something new and amusing. Cennino fluctuates between the conversational and a style that is, by today's standards, extravagantly flowery, but in many ways the book is more accessible than more recent instruction manuals. I think he is at his best when giving practical advice. His recipes still work. He gives a detailed description of how to make ultramarine from lapis lazuli, a lengthy process that he says makes suitable work for girls. He advises on the type of friends appropriate for an artist and that an easel painter may wear fine velvet. He warns against wearing paint on your face as it will make you old before your time.

He was allegedly not a great artist, although he makes bold claims for his qualifications to instruct:

I will make note of what was taught me by the aforesaid Agnolo, my master, and of what I have tried out with my own hand; first invoking High Almighty God, the father, son and Holy Ghost; then that most delightful advocate of all sinners, Virgin Mary; and of Saint Luke the Evangelist, the first Christian painter; and of my advocate Saint Eustace; and in general, of all the Saints of Paradise, AMEN.

This book is illustrated with step-by-step progressions through the processes involved in creating particular paintings and drawings, which, like Cennino, 'I have tried out with my own hand.' My efforts are not always brilliant — I am no Michelangelo — but I believe that the experience of trying things out makes for a worthwhile dialogue between then and now.

Some of the processes have been re-created specially for this book, while other reconstructions were commissioned for specific projects; all have been part of a personal exploration.

I hope that the book conveys my enthusiasm for understanding how artists made their work, and that it will encourage readers to try different materials and techniques for themselves. Above all, I hope that when readers look at paintings and drawings in museums and galleries their pleasure, understanding and admiration will be increased by knowing more about how they were made.

Drawing

Drawing

A drawing by an eight-year-old. The model is Joanna Douglas Oliver.

A drawing of a member of the House of Lords made by a fellow member during a Campaign for Drawing project

What are drawings for? Drawings are thoughts without words that may be universally understood. Drawings are used to communicate ideas and record information. A drawing may convey meaning regardless of how accomplished or unaccomplished the artist is.

In children the impetus to draw comes before we learn to write. The drawing on the left is by an eight-year-old. Below it is a drawing of a member of the House of Lords made by a fellow member during a Campaign for Drawing project. The aim of the Campaign is to make drawing a normal activity for everyone. However, it was interesting to see that a leader of the nation (who probably had not drawn very recently) could not draw any better than an eight-year-old. It was probably around the age of eight that the peer and most of his colleagues stopped drawing regularly. Sadly, the ability to draw tends to recede as writing takes over.

Artists, though, continue to learn and use drawing as part of their working practice, as they have done for centuries. Some would argue that drawing has ceased to be an essential skill for designers and artists, especially now that there are computer programmes that can take the struggle out of drawing. I feel certain, though, that drawing will not disappear as a human activity. Even those programmes had to start out as manual drawings, and I have seen award-winning architects demonstrate their ideas as a doodle. New tools like computer-aided design should be welcomed and used in addition to the instinctive need to express ideas in drawing.

Miraculously, some drawings on fragile paper and parchment have survived for hundreds of years, bearing witness to the intimate thought process of the person who made them. There are drawings that show us the particular researches an artist did into how he understood the world. There are pattern books from different periods with examples of gesture, types of people, animals and plants for artists to use as reference in their work. (Not all these were based in reality. After all, who has actually seen an angel? But the wings of a bird combined with the body of a person could be made to be one.) There are also documents, like inventories and wills, that show how one artist would specially leave a collection of drawings to another, and these would be used for study and copying.

Most made things – paintings, sculptures, dresses, buildings, cars – start life as drawings. In the past, an artist's training would involve practising drawing all the elements that might go into a picture: figures doing different actions, faces with different expressions, parts of bodies, animals and plants. Artists' apprentices practised all the time from a very young age, so that by the time they were in their teens they could draw most things from memory. Benvenuto Cellini (1500–1571) commented that: 'The teacher placed a human eye in front of poor sensitive children as their first step in copying and making portraits. At least that's what happened to me in my childhood and it probably happened to others as well.' Cennino advised the apprentice to: 'set yourself to practise drawing, drawing only a little each day, so that you may not come to lose your taste for it or get tired of it.' He also recommended practising a little and often even on holidays – and that you shouldn't fall in love with your efforts. How wise! He seems to suggest that you should always strive to do better rather than be seduced by an easy mark.

Leonardo da Vinci (1452–1519) left pages of visual explorations into anatomy, botany and machinery that were very advanced for their time. The eminent heart surgeon Francis Wells was inspired by Leonardo's drawings of the workings of the heart to moderate the way that he does a particular heart valve repair. (In a recent television programme Mr Wells demonstrated what he was doing by drawing with a patient's blood – perhaps the most extraordinary drawing material ever! It was not done to be ghoulish; it was practical in a sterile environment.)

The surviving drawings of Michelangelo (1475–1564) are wide-ranging. Personal sketches, like notes to himself, took the form of a few lines to help him understand, say, a twisting body that might end up as a 'three-dimensional drawing' in the form of a marble dying slave or the figure of a resting pope (who looks as though he is sitting

Be sure to take with you a little book with pages prepared with bone meal, and with a silverpoint briefly note the movements and actions of the bystanders and their grouping. This will teach you how to compose narrative paintings. When your book is full, put it aside and keep it for your later use, then take another book and continue as before.

Leonardo da Vinci

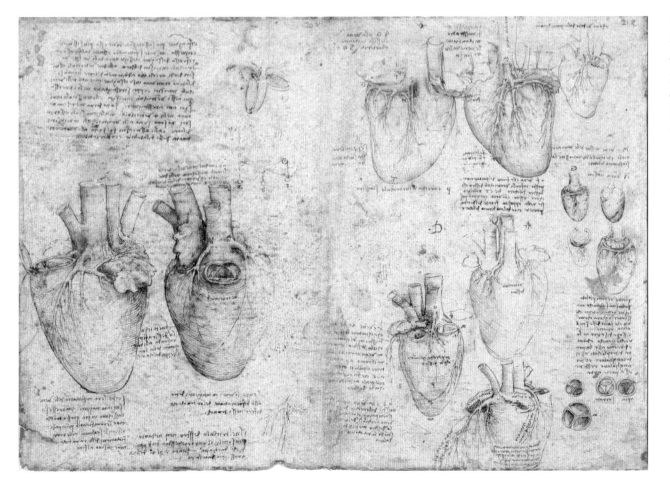

Leonardo da Vinci, *Studies of the heart*, c. 1510–13, pen and ink on blue paper Royal Library, Windsor

The manner of their attire and painting them selues when they goe to their generall huntinges, or at theire Solemne feasts.

on a lavatory) that became a grand tomb. Some of the numerous cast of characters that became giants on the Sistine Ceiling began as little drawings. Other drawings were highly finished pieces that that were given to a patron or friend. Michelangelo lived at a time when drawing was beginning to be considered as important and collectable artwork.

Before photography, drawing was essential to convey visual information. Artists were commissioned to record the world. Sometimes they accompanied the teams of travellers who explored Australia, Africa and the Americas. Their job was to record the flora and fauna of strange places as honestly as they were able.

In the sixteenth century John White (*fl.* 1577–1593) sailed to America with Sir Walter Raleigh's expedition to record the strange animals, plants and people of the New World. It was said that his drawings and paintings were also intended as an inducement to prospective settlers. Perhaps he stretched credulity a little when he portrayed the indigenous people in the poses of elegant Elizabethan courtiers (though with little or no clothing). His illustrations of fruits and animals are more honest.

Cassiano dal Pozzo (1588–1657) in the seventeenth century commissioned and collected drawings for his Paper Museum.

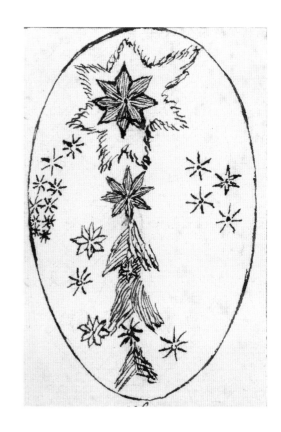

Above John White, *The manner of their attire and painting themselves,* 1585–93, watercolour and graphite touched with white on paper, 263 × 150 mm
A portrait of a member of one of the two Algonquian tribes, the Secotan and the Pomiooc, who lived in what is now Virginia and North Carolina.
British Museum, London
Right Unidentified Italian artist, *Observations made with a microscope, possibly of liquids, c.* 1626–30 Royal Library, Windsor

Attributed to Vincenzo Leonardi, *African civet*,
c. 1630, watercolour and body colour over black
chalk on paper, 344 × 476 mm
One of the drawings collected by Cassiano for his
Paper Museum
Royal Library, Windsor

The drawings cover everything that a learned person might wish to know about the world and its history. He had apparently seen drawings brought back from the New World that, although interesting, did not impress in terms of observation and aesthetic, and he was wise in his choice of artists, commissioning some of the best painters of the day, including Nicolas Poussin (1594–1665). Cassiano was a supporter of Galileo and a member of the Lincei Academy, an international club for the dissemination of new ideas. Members of the Lincei were among the first people to have access to and use of the microscope that had been invented around 1623. So they were able to investigate the world magnified, and artists recorded what was seen. In a meeting between art and science, artists and scholars pooled resources, recording, dissecting and drawing the smallest detail of life for the first time.

Ch. lunula

Sydney Parkinson, *Chaetodon lunula (raccoon butterflyfish)*, 1768–71, watercolour on paper, 250 × 325 mm Natural History Museum, London

In the eighteenth century, Sydney Parkinson (*c*. 1745–1771), who was a young artist in his twenties when he went to Australia on the *Endeavour* with Captain Cook and Sir Joseph Banks, made drawings and paintings in the most difficult conditions. Banks gave a flavour of these difficulties when he described how insects would

eat painters' colours off the paper as fast as they can be laid on, and if a fish is to be drawn there is more trouble in keeping them off [it] than in the drawing itself. Many expedients have been thought of . . . none succeed better than a mosquito net which covers chair, painter and drawings. But when that is not sufficient, a fly trap was necessary to set within this [net] to distract the vermin from eating the colours.

Parkinson did not return alive from this journey and it was two hundred years before his drawings were turned into coloured lithographs and published as a florilegium.

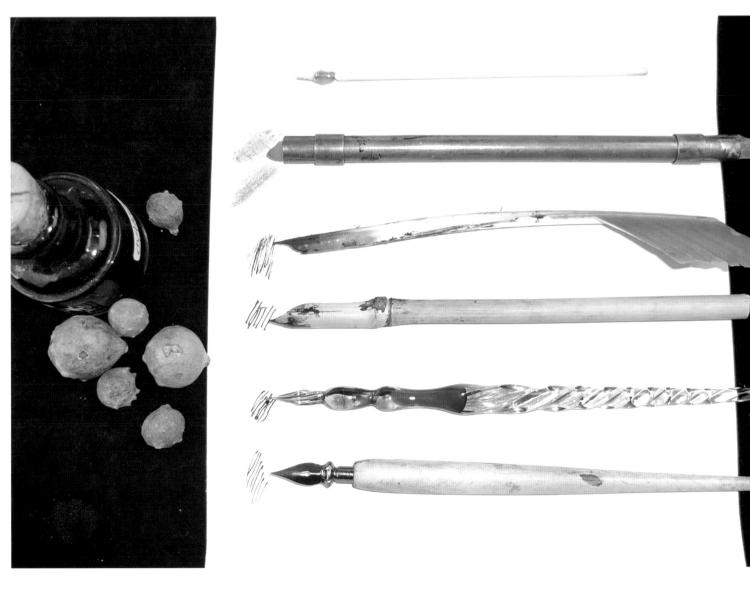

The basics

Drawings are made with a variety of tools and materials. The kind of mark a brush, reed or quill pen can make is particular to each, and whereas today we have a plethora of manufactured drawing materials of consistent quality, in the past the character of each tool, often crafted by the artist, was individual. Before industrialization, which introduced some quality control, paper, parchment and other materials like charcoal, chalks and inks could also vary greatly from batch to batch. Various chalks and types of charcoal were used over the centuries, many of them sourced locally.

There are few records to tell us of the pleasures or frustrations of using these materials, but one can imagine how they might work, or try them out to gain an insight. A badly cut pen or one that is too hard or too soft is very annoying and holds up the drawing process. A brittle piece of chalk that doesn't maintain a point could make you want to throw it at the wall.

Above left Ink and the oak galls from which it was made

Above right, top to bottom Silverpoint stylus; *porte-crayon* with red chalk at one end and black at the other; quill pen; reed pen; Venetian glass pen; pen with steel nib

A black chalk drawing of a male
nude, after Michelangelo

Materials

Chalks

Natural chalks occur in various colours in different parts of the world. The black chalk
used by Leonardo and Michelangelo, which mostly came from Piedmont, is blacker
than the more brownish chalk available across the Alps to Albrecht Durer (1471–1528).
The various chalks became very popular in the sixteenth century, perhaps because they
are so versatile, much more so than pen or silverpoint. They can be used to make fine
lines as well as for smudged, soft modelling. Leonardo recommended black chalk to
Michelangelo as being more useful for subtle effects than red chalk and less smudgy than
charcoal. Red chalk is not red but a rusty iron colour from a geological mix of the
mineral hematite and clay. Hematite could provide a red pigment for paint when
ground fine enough. Mixed with red clay it became soft enough to be used for drawing.
The hardness of chalk varied greatly. Today it is difficult to find natural black drawing
chalk but red is still available.

Charcoal

Thin twigs of willow are roasted slowly until they are black. They can be made in
varying thickness and hardness. Although charcoal is very brittle it can be used to make
bold dark marks, fine lines and smudges. Charcoal drawings are forever vulnerable to
accidental smudges.

Graphite

A mineral found in Europe and used as it is or pulverized, mixed with clay and encased
in wood to form a pencil. Nowadays graphite pencils are called lead pencils, but before
the eighteenth century a pencil would have been understood to be a fine-pointed brush,
and a lead pencil a lead stylus for drawing with, as in metalpoint.

Left Red chalk drawng of the hand of God, after a drawing in Michelangelo's sketchbook

Below Michelangelo, *Archers shooting at a herm*, c. 1530, red chalk on paper, 219 × 323 mm

Royal Library, Windsor

Inks

There are many recipes for inks. Ingredients such as soot, roasted peach and almond kernels, carbonized cereals, rice and barley would all produce black ink. Sepia from cuttlefish gave brown ink. Hawthorn wood boiled in an iron pot produced an iron tannate. Bistre was boiled wood soot. Iron gall ink was made from oak galls, iron sulphate and gum arabic, combined either hot or cold. The gum only acted as a thickener to make the ink less watery. When ink is first made it gives a grey mark that develops to deep black in minutes. Over decades the black ink oxidizes to brown. Sometimes the acidity of the ink is so strong that it has eaten through the paper. Indian ink was actually from China and made from burnt pork fat and oil. Binders for the black colouring matter include saliva, gum, oil and glue.

Pastels

These are pigments bound with china clay, gum tragacanth and water, and are used for a method of dry painting that became popular in the eighteenth century. The hardness of the stick can be regulated by the strength of the gum. Pastels are also made with oil and wax.

Sanguine

A crayon of red clay.

Tools

Brushes

The brushes used for drawing and making thin washes with diluted ink or paint were the same as those used for painting. Small brushes for drawing were usually made from the tail hairs of small animals like stoat, sable, weasel or squirrel. The hairs needed to be strong and resistant to water. (For more on brushes, see pages 130–32.)

Erasers

Kneaded lumps of bread, leather strips and dried cuttlefish were all used as erasers. They worked by absorbing the deposit or abrading the surface of the paper.

Fixative

Milk was recommended as a fixative for drawings, to prevent them smudging, but how it was applied is a mystery. One would think that it should be sprayed somehow.

Metalpoint/silverpoint

These terms describe drawing with a metal stylus, which could be made from silver, gold or lead. The metalpoint tool was sometimes fashioned by a jewellery maker, or it might be just a simple metal wire attached to a stick. The mark is achieved by a tiny amount of metal being deposited on paper that has been primed with pigment; often hatched strokes are used. There is a reaction between the paint and the metal and a delicate grey line is produced. Over years the line will oxidize and change from grey to brown.

This method of drawing was used during medieval and Renaissance times. It looks delicate and is unforgiving as a process. Cennino recommended that artists master the

Leonardo da Vinci,
Head of a warrior,
c. 1475–80, silverpoint on
paper, 287 × 211 mm
British Museum, London

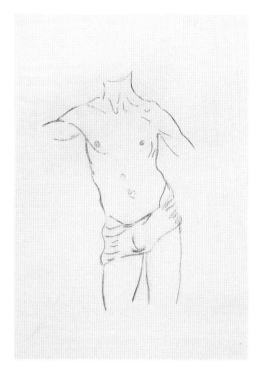
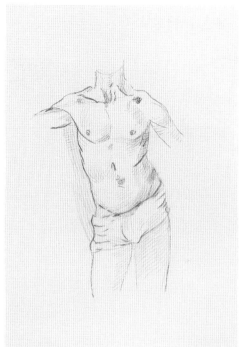
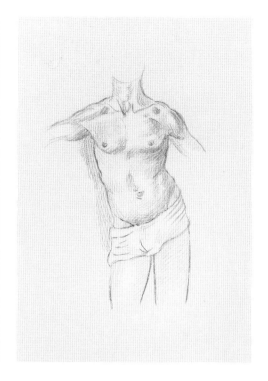

Three stages of a drawing in silverpoint on pink paper, after Lorenzo di Credi

difficult technique of metalpoint drawing before graduating to pen and ink.

A tinted ground layer could be used instead of white. The pink-tinted paper in my imitation of Lorenzo di Credi, above, serves as the middle tone, allowing for white highlights of chalk or paint to give the figure a more three-dimensional look. Many metalpoint drawings are on papers tinted pink, blue or green. The tint was created by applying a wash of transparent or opaque paint made from plant dyes.

Metalpoint drawings might also be done on a reusable surface, created by applying a water-soluble paint on paper or on the surface of a little panel of wood (see page 27). This allowed apprentices to practise, as if they were not satisfied lines on the soluble surface could be moistened, dissolving the paint and thus erasing the lines, and the surface dried for further use. Some scholars think that the use of this method accounts for the paucity of surviving drawings by very young masters.

Metalpoint drawings – most often silverpoint – could be given to an engraver to copy. They are also found as the base for drawings that were then inked over, and on the gesso ground of egg tempera paintings.

Pens

Quill pens were cut from feathers. The best feathers – because the strongest and most pliable – were goose, raven, swan or duck. The feather should be mature enough to drop from the bird rather than being plucked from the wing. A quill from the left side of the bird would be better for a right-handed person and vice versa. The quill could be cut to suit the kind of mark to be made – chiselled for calligraphy and pointed for drawing. The flexibility of the feather meant that the amount of pressure exerted would vary the thickness of the line and the darkness. A disadvantage of the quill was the need to sharpen frequently.

Quill and ink drawing on laid paper, after Michelangelo

Artists of the Renaissance period were accustomed to using pen and ink from an early age and the impressive hatching strokes, as individual as handwriting, make it very difficult to fake a drawing. The hatched strokes of early Michelangelo drawings, learnt in his early training with Ghirlandaio, are so sculptural; the hatching seems to caress the form. All the strokes combine to produce the finished shape. My drawing after Michelangelo is made with a quill and ink. Trying to emulate him is a lesson, and very challenging if you haven't been trained from an early age. It is compulsive, a bit like knitting, but it is really hard to match the sureness of stroke without its looking wobbly.

It is interesting when examining drawings of the period that there is rarely a tail at the end of a stroke. In a later forgery the end of the stroke often has an upward tick that

Above left Raphael, *Studies for the Virgin and Child, c.* 1505–8, pen and ink on paper, 253 × 183 mm
British Museum, London
Right Eric Hebborn, forgery of Raphael's *Studies for the Virgin and Child*, pen and ink on paper, 253 × 183 mm

is not usually present in old master drawings. I think this tail is the giveaway mark of the fake drawing – that and the number of strokes. A discerning eye should be able to recognize the nuances of stroke, particularly in the endings, and make comparison by counting strokes. (On the other hand, a sensible forger would not choose to copy a particular drawing but rather do a 'style of'.) Eric Hebborn (1934–1996) was a successful forger of drawings until his untimely and suspicious death. His drawing after Raphael is pretty good when you compare it with the real one in the British Museum, but if you make a comparison of counted lines and look at the ends of the strokes they don't match up. The Madonna's face does not have the same curve on the side.

Reed pens can be made from any dry stiff reed or bamboo. The end is cut into a nib shape. It is not always possible to tell the difference between a reed and a quill mark. Certainly many an artist, including Rembrandt, used both. The difference seems to be in the quality of the stroke. The reed, being harder than the quill, can retain its point for longer. Both reed and quill can be used for really fine or thick lines. Most people would

Left Raphael, *The Virgin and Child with an Angel*,
1498–1520, pen and brown ink on paper,
205 × 225 mm
British Museum, London
Below Rembrandt, *A Farmstead by a Stream*,
1562–3, reed pen and brown ink on paper,
109 × 221 mm
Private collection

say that variable pressure with a quill will give a more varied line, but a varied line is also possible with a reed.

Steel pens The steel nib replaced the quill in the nineteenth century. Some nibs were very ornate. Joseph Gillot adapted the techniques he used to manufacture buttons to the making of flexible steel nibs. The sharpness of the steel nib encouraged paper manufacturers to produce paper with a smoother, harder finish to suit the new pens.

Penknife

A small knife was used for the difficult skill of cutting pens from feathers or dried and hardened reeds. We don't know whether artists of the past endlessly sharpened their quills or delegated the task to an assistant or apprentice. There is a story – probably apocryphal – that in ancient China a little monkey was trained to bring pens to the artist and that it was chained to the desk. Whoever carried out this job would obviously need to know what the master wanted, as the thickness of the nib would dictate the kind of line. Being natural products, quill and reed pens vary. They can become soggy from use but I have come across no reference to a need for a plentiful supply. Certainly the requirement for frequent sharpening allows for thinking time. By the eighteenth century mechanical pen-cutters were being manufactured. They were rather like cigar-cutters.

Drawing surfaces

Panels

Small wooden panels with a gesso ground were often used in the fourteenth and fifteenth centuries, for drawing on and particularly for practising.

Paper

The early manufacture of paper is ascribed to the Chinese around the first century AD. The word paper stems from papyrus. The distinction between papyrus and paper as we know it is that papyrus is made from plant fibres pounded and layered in a process comparable to lamination, while paper is usually made from rags that have been pulped, pulverized and squashed on to a tray mould that has a layer of wires or thin bamboo attached to it. (For more on the process of papermaking, see pages 126–8.) Until the twelfth century European paper was manufactured predominantly in Spain, whose primacy was, however, superseded by Italy in the fifteenth century. Fabriano, an Italian paper-manufacturing company established in the sixteenth century, still exists. Rags from linen and/or cotton make the finest and strongest paper for drawing and watercolour. Paper manufacturing required a lot of water and older factories are still often sited by a river. (The ground near the Whatman factory in Kent still throws up buttons from the clothes that became the rags that became paper.)

In the Renaissance period, it was not uncommon to have tinted papers of blue, green, grey or pink. The colour was created either by using coloured rags in the pulp, which created an integral tint, or by applying a wash of colour from a vegetable dye such as indigo blue as a surface coat. The colour of the paper could be used to create a half-tone for artists

who wished to use white chalk or painted highlights to give a more sculptural, three-dimensional quality to a drawing. Pure white paper did not exist until the discovery of bleach in the nineteenth century. Today there are thousands of different types and colours of paper for artists to choose from. There are still some small manufacturers who produce handmade papers but these days the majority of papers are made by machine.

Parchment and vellum

The use of parchment and vellum evolved in ancient Roman times. Parchment was usually the skin of a goat or sheep, stretched and scraped (see page 40). Vellum, usually made from calfskin, was finer: even today it is reserved for very special documents. There are stories that the finest, thinnest vellum was made from the skin of aborted or stillborn calves, but opinion these days suggests that this may simply be a way of describing the extreme fineness of the skin. Another theory is that it could be from the skin of smaller animals. A researcher at the Victoria and Albert Museum, Timea Tallian, who has done wonderful work investigating and reconstructing miniatures, has actually made some parchment from mouse skin!

Taffelet

The taffelet was an erasable drawing table made from paper, parchment or board coated with pigment – usually white – bound with gum arabic or saliva. You could draw on it using a silver or lead stylus (see page 20). Cennino recommended the reusable drawing tablet for practising, the idea being that you should not use more expensive paper until your drawing was of sufficient quality. The taffelet could be used for drawing on the spot and then developing in the studio or for handing on to an engraver.

Right A perforated cartoon, after Raphael
Far right The cartoon pounced through and
partially inked in

Drawing aids

Cartoons

The word cartoon comes from the Italian word for paper, *cartone*. Cartoon is a general
name applied to a drawing used to transfer an image. Usually, a drawing by the master
would be perforated and charcoal dust would be pounced (rubbed) through the holes,
leaving a dotty drawing on the panel or wall. A variation of this is known as *spolvero*, a
method in which a tracing of a drawing is perforated and pounced through; this method
preserves the original drawing. A cartoon is usually the same size as the image of the
prospective painting. Because of the limitation of the size of paper, cartoons were often

Take note that before going any further, I will give you the exact proportions of a man. Those of a woman I will disregard, for she does not have any set proportion.
Cennino Cennini, *Il Libro dell'Arte*, late fourteenth century

made from several sheets of paper pasted together. The same drawing could be used repeatedly. There are some cartoons to be found in museum collections where the perforations can be seen. For example, they are visible in a large image of Henry VIII by Holbein in the National Portrait Gallery in London, and in a Michelangelo cartoon of the Madonna and Child in the British Museum.

Another method of transfer, described by Vasari, involves interleaving a charcoal-dusted sheet placed face down on the surface to be painted, with the original drawing on top. A metal stylus is then used to press the design on to the surface. This method preserves the top copy for longer than a pricked and pounced cartoon and can produce a more subtle result, as shading can be incorporated.

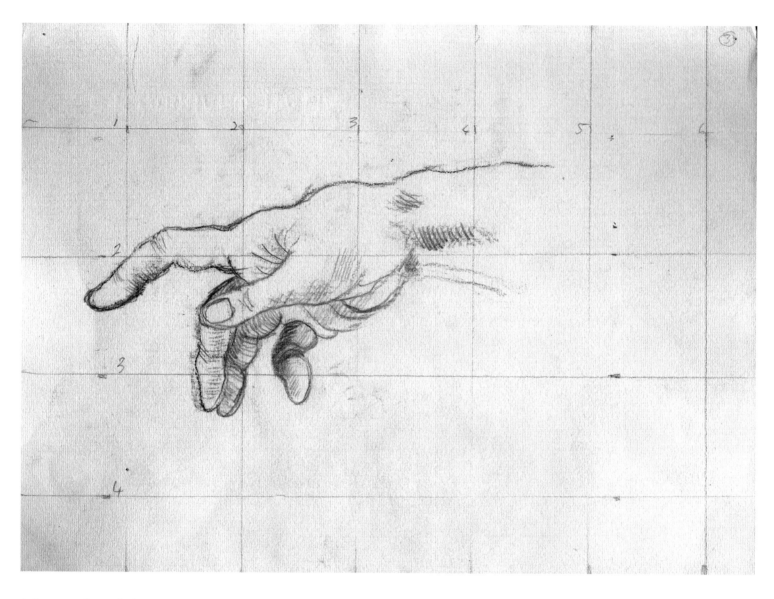

A drawing with a grid of squares on top, ready
for enlarging

Grids

To enlarge or reduce an image a grid can be drawn on the original drawing and a larger
or smaller grid drawn on the surface to which the image is to be transferred. The same
number of squares is required but enlarged or reduced in proportion.

To help with this, artists sometimes used a see-through framed grid. The paper would
have a matching grid, with the same number of squares, proportionately larger or
smaller. When looking through the grid it is helpful to close one eye. If you are careful
to keep your head in the same position, it is possible to map out what can be seen
through the grid by following the image square by square. The grid frame is also an aid
to drawing in perspective.

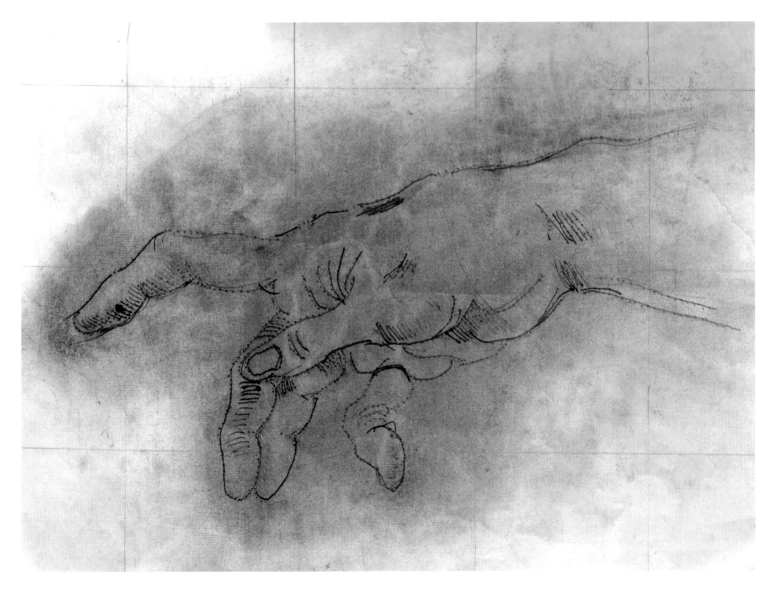

A larger drawing taken from the smaller one by
enlarging the grid

Right A draped wax model and a drawing of a draped figure
Below Flying wax cherub and drawing

Lay figures

These were wooden models with articulated joints that could be dressed and posed. They could be small or life-size.

Wax and clay figures

These were used to practise drawing figures in different poses. Drapery folds were sometimes created by dipping fabric in plaster or glue and arranging folds draped over the figures. This goes some way to explain why the elaborate arrangements of draperies in early paintings tend to look static and overly complex.

Leonardo da Vinci, *Study of drapery for a kneeling figure*, c. 1496, lamp black heightened with white on blueish paper, 213 × 159 mm
Royal Library, Windsor

Illuminated
manuscripts

Illuminated manuscripts

In his excellent concise book *The Materials and Techniques of Medieval Painting*, Daniel V. Thompson describes the medieval scribes and illuminators as engaged in the 'greatest of all medieval arts'. Today, art is a highly commercial commodity and some artists have celebrity status; the personality of the artist sometimes seems more important than the art. It is perhaps hard for us to comprehend the skill, devotion and – on the whole – anonymity of the medieval artist. Thompson suggests that the small size of this work and the fact that it was not displayed on walls has led to illuminated manuscript being considered a lesser art compared to larger, grander schemes. But look a little deeper, preferably with a magnifying glass, and you will enter a world of large ideas on a small scale. Plants, beasts real and imagined, gold and rich colours are used to embellish script so carefully wrought that one might think that the angels often displayed in the pages must have made them. The words were there to inspire not just with their content but also through their beautifully executed letters and decorations.

Although there are excellent reproductions of some of these books there is no substitute for holding in your hand a fourteenth-century book of hours. These were little books containing handwritten religious writings and prayers to punctuate the day, produced for private use. It is hard to convey the excitement of turning the pages of such an exquisite document. Alongside texts to contemplate and inspire are decorations and narrative pictures to emphasize the words or in some cases just to be beautiful. The gold shines and the colours are mostly still bright because the pages have not been constantly exposed to light.

The pages were made to last by scribes and illuminators whose working methods and materials are the subject of ongoing speculation and study. The quality of written sources before printing was dependent on the diligence and knowledge of the scribe. Handwritten treatises, often copies of copies, have perhaps in some instances become like the repetition in a game of Chinese whispers. They contain inaccuracies. Measurements are often vague: how big, for example, is half a walnut or hazelnut shell? Some instructions suggest 'continue stirring until it is good' – a difficult concept to interpret. None the less, these treatises make informative reading and give practical instruction that with some knowledge and imagination can be followed today.

We tend to think of monks making these books but there was also an international business that flourished in secular workshops, competing for the most illustrious patrons: beautiful books were made for those who could afford the best. Artists from different countries were favoured at different times, according to fashion. Jean Foucquet (*c.* 1420–1478) and Jean Bourdichon (*c.* 1457–1521) were perhaps as sought after as Michelangelo or Leonardo. Both served the royal families of France as illuminators.

The writings of Christine de Pisan (1365–1430) are a good example of work that needed a new kind of illustration. She wrote non-religious tracts and poetry: most famously, *The Treasures of the City of Ladies*, an innovative survival guide for women. It was unusual at this time for a woman to be a writer who made a living by her pen. An early

Jean Bourdichon, *The Virgin of the
Annunciation*, from the *Hours of Henry VII*,
c. 1500, watercolour on parchment,
240 × 170 mm
British Library, London

Christine de Pisan in her study, writing 'Cent Ballades', 1410–11, watercolour on parchment
British Library, London

Below left Jean Bourdichon (attrib.), *Christ Carrying the Cross to Calvary with the Virgin and Soldiers*, from *Book of Hours, Use of Tours*, sixteenth century, watercolour on parchment, 145 × 90 mm
British Library, London

Below right Spanish School, *Christ Carrying His Cross*, 1670–80, oil on canvas, 2273 × 1317 mm
Dulwich Picture Gallery, London

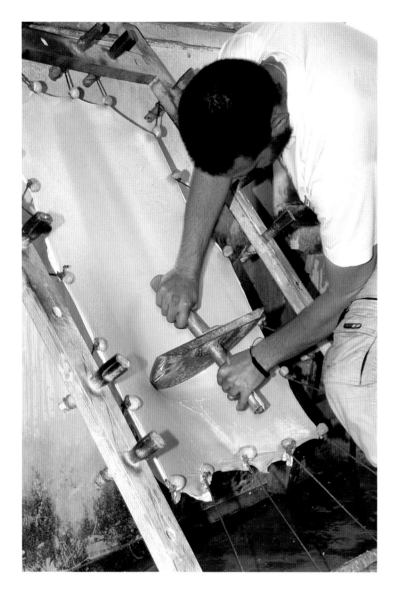

Preparing parchment

Above left Using a moon-shaped blade to thin the skin

Above right Parchment with powdered sandarac and the pounce bag
used for its application

feminist, after she was widowed she was able to maintain herself
by writing rather than remarrying or entering a convent. She had
opinions on the skill and behaviour of artists too. She allegedly
described Parisian scribes and illuminators as the best, but was
disappointed by their 'excessive indulgence in luxury that brings
misfortune on them'. (*Plus ça change!*)

Most of the books and manuscripts were made on parchment.
Parchment is animal skin that has been worked until it is thin and
smooth enough to be a surface on which fine lettering and painting
may be made. It is very durable. Vellum is considered finer than
parchment and usually comes from calfskin.

The process of illumination

Preparation

The procedure for preparing parchment and making it into a
book changed little until the invention of mechanical printing.
The skin of freshly killed animals was soaked for days in water
and lime, a caustic alkali that softens and loosens the hairs on the
skin. The skin was then rinsed and stretched on a frame. Once
stretched tight, the skin was scraped to remove the hairs and
then thinned to the desired thickness, using a moon-shaped blade
to avoid a point tearing the skin. Next it was trimmed into sheets
and folded into folios, and the edges were cut to make pages.

Sometimes pumice was rubbed over the surface to give a
smoother finish and fill the pores of the skin. Pumice (which

was imported into England) was not considered as good for smoothing as the manufactured material Thompson described as a 'bread' made from ground glass, yeast and flour that was then baked. This would be rubbed over the surface. (Hopefully nobody ate it for lunch.)

Also recommended for making the surface receptive to paint and inks was the application of powdered sandarac. This is a hard resin also used to make varnish. Tim Noad, a heraldic artist who uses many traditional techniques, told me that he uses a sprinkle of sandarac, pumice and grated cuttlefish. He rubs it over the surface of the parchment with the aid of a parchment offcut, and then sweeps away the excess powder with a feather or brush.

Manuscripts were often worked on both sides of the skin, but it is preferable to use the outside or hair side.

Design

Most manuscripts, especially if they were to be decorated, were a collaboration between the scribe and the illuminator. Very distinct techniques were involved.

The scribe was responsible for the overall design, deciding on the position of the lines and the spaces for the decorative initials and pictures. He mapped out the pages carefully, using a variety of methods, including incising lines with a metal stylus, silver- or leadpoint. These lines may also have been strengthened with brown or black ink applied with a quill. The ink was sometimes coloured (but faint), and the margins were generous to accommodate jottings and mucky fingerprints. Multiple lines could be economically indicated through several pages by piercing the pages through with a metal point so that when the page was turned the marks were there, ready to be joined up as lines. In areas where there were to be pictures and decorations the scribe sometimes left instructions. Mostly these have been eradicated but there are some unfinished manuscripts to be seen in museums and libraries where informal little notes of instruction or doodles survive. The scribe used a carefully cut quill and ink to write the text before the illuminator set to work in the spaces that had been reserved.

The training of illuminators, like that of other artists, was about the emulation of a master, not originality. There were pattern books to follow containing flora, fauna and alphabets, which can be seen over the centuries and across disciplines. So one sometimes sees similar designs and decorations appearing in larger formats such as fresco, panel and canvas and in miniature in books and manuscripts. Designs were easily adapted from the patterns for books, as parchment was translucent and easy to trace through. Once traced, the pattern could also be pricked and pounced like a cartoon or embroidery design. As well as the standardized forms for letters, flora and fauna, there were also, of course, exceptions that required invention.

Once the page had been designed and the text had been inscribed, the next step was to prepare any areas where gold was to be used. Gold was applied before the colours because the process of gilding was messy and the featherweight gold leaf might stick to other areas.

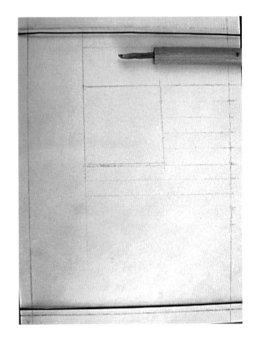

Mapping out the page, with a lead stylus

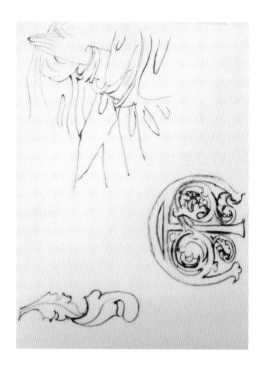

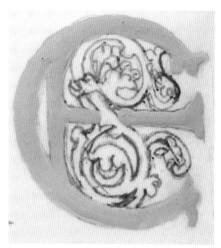

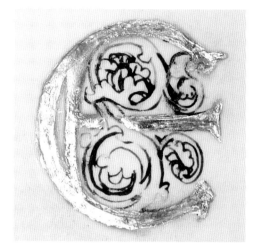

Designs for initial E, Madonna's robe and leaf, incised with stylus and reinforced with quill and ink

The initial with a pink gesso ground applied as a base for the gold

The gilded initial

Gold leaf on a gilder's cushion, with a cutting knife and a long-haired brush

With blue added   With added malachite green and brasilwood red With a background of cochineal red

Gilding

Gold has been used for writing and decoration for thousands of years. The gilded page draws attention to particular areas and seduces the reader to turn the page, in anticipation of the next visual feast. Even today, with all our sophisticated printing processes, it is not possible to synthesize gold on the page in a way that compares to the real thing applied by a skilled artist.

There are many recipes in treatises describing methods for application of gold, but the two basic methods of gilding are drawing or painting with gold ink or paint; and applying gold leaf to flat or raised surfaces.

Gold ink and paint were made by combining powdered gold – called shell gold, because it was often stored in cake form, in a mussel shell – and a sticky binder of gum, or egg white (glair) and water. The gum came from the sap of various plants; the plant was usually described as gum arabic but it could be acacia, tragacanth or senegal. Glair is made by thinning egg white by beating it to a stiff froth and leaving it to stand. The liquid that forms underneath is less viscous than the egg white was before; it is this thinner egg white or albumen that is the medium.

Flat areas of gold leaf work required something sticky for the gold to adhere to. The illuminator painted a glue or gum where the gold was to go, endeavouring to leave no brushmark, as any unevenness of the surface would show through the thin gold. The aqueous adhesive was allowed to dry and then, to reactivate the stickiness, the illuminator would breathe on it just before laying the gold. This process requires great dexterity on the part of the artist, and the right humidity in the air. A damp day is good for gilding.

A burnisher made from a baby tooth

A stylized leaf from a model book
From top to bottom The outline of the leaf,
with shell gold paint; the leaf with added
ultramarine with a red glaze; with a brasilwood
red background

The praying Madonna has a brasilwood red gown and ultramarine overmantel. The highlights are shell gold.

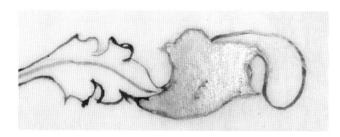

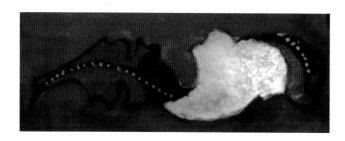

Raised gilding, laid on a surface of gesso, was sometimes applied under gold initials at the beginning of a sentence or paragraph or for a particular name. Before punctuation acquired complex rules it was a way of making a word stand out as important. The gesso for a raised gilded letter was different from the base for raised gilding on wooden panel paintings of the same period (see page 83). This is because of the nature of the skin from which the book's pages were made. The gilding on a page must be able to withstand movement, as pages are turned frequently and some elasticity must be built into the mixture to allow for flexibility. There are many recipes for gesso on parchment but basically it is composed of fine plaster, a little red earth, glue (either animal or vegetable) and a plasticizer such as sugar or honey. It was dribbled on to the surface with either a brush or quill, the aim being to produce a flawless base for the gold. A piece of gold leaf was cut and laid on a leather cushion. Once the gesso was dry the glue was drawn to the surface by the application of warm breath, while at the same moment the gold was lifted from the cushion with a special flat, long-haired brush, in such a way that it leaped from the brush to the damp surface. Excess gold was brushed away and after further drying the raised letter could be burnished to a brilliant shine with a small burnisher made from an animal's tooth or a polished agate (for my example I used a burnisher made from one of my children's baby teeth!). Flat gilding, without gesso, is not so shiny.

Applying colour

After the text and the gold had been applied to the page the coloured decorations and pictures would be added. Some are narrative, with decorative borders and initials or reference for plants and animals real or imagined.

The outlines of the design would be coloured in with a variety of natural paints from animal, plant and mineral sources. Different binders might be used for particular colours on the same illustration. Treatises recommended egg white for mineral colours and vegetable gum for vegetable colours. The vegetable colours – derived from dyes that had been precipitated, washed and dried before having a binder added – were thin and tended to tint parchment. (For more on pigments, see pages 150–53.)

Clothlets: a way of storing colours by dyeing fabric but not fixing the dye; the colour could be reconstituted by steeping in gum water.

Natural colours
From left to right Greens – verdigris, malachite; reds – brasilwood, madder, cochineal, vermilion; blue – ultramarine; yellow – buckthorn berry; green – mixed from buckthorn yellow and ultramarine blue

Minerals
From left to right Malachite, two pieces of vermilion, orpiment, polished lapis lazuli, unpolished lapis, azurite

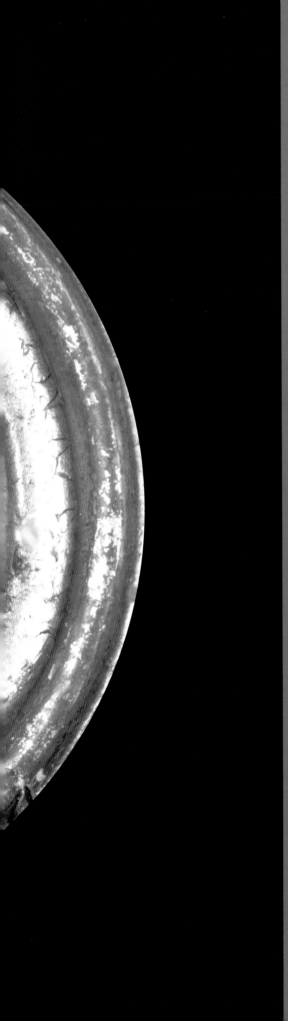

Miniatures

Miniatures

Miniatures are small jewel-like pictures, usually portraits. The golden age of miniature painting was the sixteenth century, when the miniature portrait or scene was a rather English speciality. The reigns of Henry VIII and Elizabeth I produced a great flowering of these tiny works, perhaps in part because of the subject restrictions imposed on artists during the upheavals in Christianity during the Reformation. Overtly iconic subject matter for visual art was unacceptable in countries that broke away from the domination of the Church of Rome, and in England vast amounts of art deemed to have the 'wrong' imagery was destroyed. Small art, however, flourished unchallenged in the form of manuscript illumination. The manuscripts sometime featured portraits of patrons and it was perhaps as a development of this that the portrait miniature became an important and desirable artefact on it own. Thus the art of illuminating, with its emphasis on fine detail and elaborate designs, is said to have been the origin of the portrait miniature.

There was also an influx of foreign artists to England, some of whom were escaping persecution. They hoped to earn a living in a competitive market that was protective, via the guilds, of native artists – for example, foreign artists were not permitted to live within the city walls. However, foreign artists arriving with a reputation or personal recommendations were engaged by the court: in particular Lucas Horenbout, often known in England as Hornbolte (*c.* 1490–1543), Lavina Teerlinc (1515–1576) and, the most famous, Hans Holbein the Younger (*c.* 1497–1543). At this time artists were often multi-disciplined, producing paintings, designing decorative schemes for pageants and parties, and doing silver and gold work. Some artists were also skilled in illumination.

Nicholas Hilliard (1547–1619) was an English artist who epitomized the art of the Tudor miniature, becoming the most notable exponent of the genre. He is the first English artist whose life we know something about. He was born in the year that Henry VIII died and nearly five years after the death of Holbein. Until the age of ten he lived in Exeter with his family. He went to Europe with the Bodley family during the ten-year reign of Catholic Mary I. As a prominent Protestant family the Hilliards did well to send their son away from trouble and to gain a 'European' education. It was during this time that he would have seen and learned from fine examples of the art of illumination and absorbed the influence of artists like Holbein and Durer.

Some time before 1624 (the date of the only manuscript, in a copyist's hand, now in Edinburgh University Library), Hilliard wrote a treatise on *The Art of Limning* that was the culmination of his experience. The word limning comes from the Latin *illuminare*, to illuminate. The treatise gives instruction for the best conditions, including lighting, the artist's distance from the sitter, the advantage of wearing silk clothes that won't shed fluff and most importantly: 'Take heed of the dandruff of the head shedding from the hair, and of speaking over your work for sparkling, for the least sparing of spittle will never be helped if it light in the face, or any part of the naked.' He lists the suitable colours and describes the sequence and processes involved in creating these tiny masterpieces.

Sixty or so years after Hilliard's *Art of Limning*, Edward Norgate (1581–1650) wrote another treatise on limning, *Miniatura* (the word miniature comes from *minium*, the red

Nicholas Hilliard, *Self-portrait at the age of thirty*, 1577, watercolour on vellum, diameter 41 mm
Victoria and Albert Museum, London

lead colour used for some letters). Norgate was a civil servant, serving James I, Charles I and the Earl of Arundel, and a polymath: a musician, herald, limner and linguist. He was appointed Windsor Herald by Arundel, who was Earl Marshal of the College of Heralds. (The College of Arms still exists to grant coats of arms and as the repository of the genealogy of families eligible to have their own coat of arms; its officers are heralds.) Norgate's skill as an heraldic artist is evidence of his artistic ability. His treatise on limning covers the same ground as Hilliard's. Both Hilliard and Norgate thought that limning was a most gentlemanly art.

Norgate's *Miniatura* is not just a practical guide but also an interpretation, and to some extent pays homage to Hilliard and his pupil Isaac Oliver. Scholars are still trying to understand some aspects of these treatises. Early editions of Norgate state that some processes or ingredients were secret, most particularly the special way that Hilliard developed to depict gems. Norgate says that he received this information in code and, although he mentions how to make the gems, experiments to emulate the effect have proved unsuccessful.

The highly vulnerable nature of seventeenth-century miniatures removes the possibility of the kind of robust investigation that is possible with tougher oil-painted surfaces, and there is still much to be understood about how these paintings were made. Interpretations by recent scholars – notably the late V. J. Murrell, Katie Coombe, Alan Derbyshire and Timea Tallian) – are more useful than the treatises for those who wish to know what it may have been like to make an Elizabethan miniature. My own experience raises a few questions. How did the binding medium for the paint used in this watercolour technique vary? Wasn't there a risk of disturbing previous layers when more than one is required? When the treatises say that the first stage of the painting was to create a carnation (flesh colour) followed by hatching to describe the form, one wonders how the carnation is not disturbed. I have not been able to discover the strength of the binder (gum arabic and sometimes a bit of sugar candy and occasionally ear wax).

Forward planning was essential, as were cleanliness, discipline and patience.

The painting was to end up as a 'jewell', to be housed in a beautiful locket. These paintings were very personal, kept about the person or in a cabinet (Elizabeth I had a collection of likenesses of her favourites).

Painting a miniature

The tablet

The surface on which the miniature was painted was known as the tablet. In the sixteenth and seventeenth centuries miniatures were usually painted on parchment or vellum. As the skin was thin and slightly transparent, to make it opaque and stiff it needed to be attached to thicker parchment or to pasteboard, made from laminated rag paper layers glued with starch paste. (In its thicker form pasteboard was used as back boards for books.) Playing cards were often used as the pasteboard support, as can be seen on the reverse of some miniatures. It would have been crucial to get the layers of pasteboard and skin to bond without warping. The side of the parchment or vellum where the hair had been was the side to paint on.

The picture was generally painted within a rectangular tablet and cut to shape, usually into a round or oval, when it was finished. Painting the miniature within a larger shape enabled the artist to handle the picture without touching the paint. However, once the painting was finished all could be lost, as the vibration of cutting could cause the background to flake off; the consistency of the binder would be crucial to the success of this process. My own efforts and those of other reconstruction students have involved a number of failures. There seem to be no descriptions of how the cutting out was done. Miniatures are sealed in cases or frames with glass or crystal protecting the face of the painting. It would perhaps be best to have the case ready for the picture to be held in, so that once the painting was finished and dry it couldn't move or be handled or exposed to the atmosphere.

First the carnation, or flesh colour, was painted, using thin opaque paint, in an approximate head shape. Hilliard cleverly suggests having a few tablets with carnation ready to suit the different complexions of potential sitters, rather like a shade card for make-up.

Both Hilliard and Norgate suggest placing the sitter at a convenient distance in a room with a constant north light. It was also important to keep containers of clean water for mixing colours and washing brushes (then known as pencils).

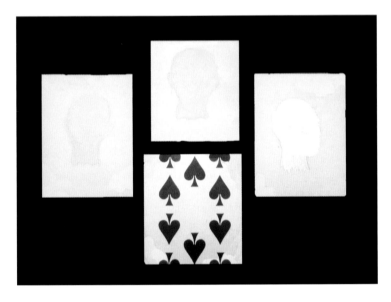

Playing cards were often used as a backing for the parchment

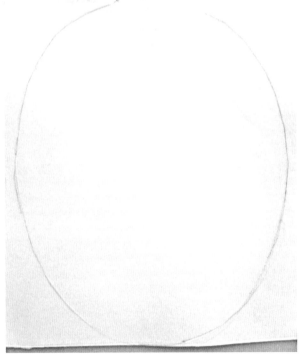

Drawing out the shape of the miniature on the parchment

Drawing in

Over the dry carnation the artist mapped out the outlines of the face and clothes with fine lines of pale red or brown watercolour. Sometimes this was done with umber, white and indigo. This was followed by what Hilliard and Norgate call 'sad colour'– very finely hatched lines to describe the form, like the hatching of engraving or fine drawing. Both writers suggest that it is better to work from light to dark, as it is difficult, even impossible, to add lightness but it is possible to go darker.

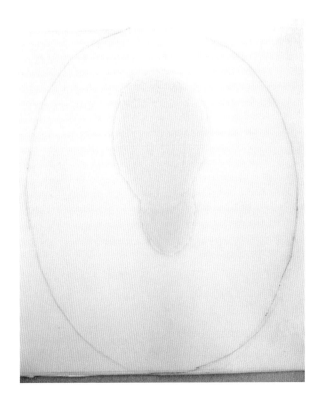

Head shape painted in carnation (flesh colour)

The sequence of creating a miniature

Over the dry carnation the outlines of the face and clothes are mapped out in pale red or brown watercolour; this is followed by very finely hatched lines to describe the form.

A first layer of azurite is thinly applied as an appetizer for the following layer.

A second layer is applied before the first is dry, so that it forms a homogeneous film with no visible brushstrokes or glitter.

Features such as hair and clothes are blocked in.

The ruff and other details are refined.

More details are added.

The blue background

Hilliard was not the first artist to adopt the plain blue background typical of early miniatures but it is in his treatise that its application is described. Some of Holbein's miniatures have a blue background that was probably applied in a similar way.

Hilliard and Norgate suggest that having painted the carnation the artist should apply blue background thus: 'grind the azurite with a muller on a slab. Mix with the binder in a shell. It should be quite liquid. Brush the colour round the edges of the figure and over the rest of the tablet. Before it is dry "float" a large and well loaded brush over the surface and leave to dry.' This really means that, having made a puddle of colour sufficient for the area, you gently apply it first to the background areas; then, before it is dry, you take another loaded brush of the mixture and apply it to the first layer, so that it forms a homogeneous film with no brushstrokes, or glitter from the sugar candy content of the binder. The first application serves as an 'appetizer' for the richer

Above Azurite for the blue background, puddled in a mussel shell

The finished miniature, with its gems, is cut to an oval, ready to be framed.

My attempt at making a gem on a gold base, using sugar and gum as a binder

next layer. It is very important to get the timing right because if the colour is not wet enough the brushstrokes will show. This is to be avoided at all costs.

Hilliard recommends reserving a brush for the sole purpose of applying the blue, which makes sense as the minerals azurite and lapis lazuli, from which the blue was made, were very costly materials. In my experience it is possible to extract residue of the paint from the brush and the mixture in the shell by floating in water and allowing the paint to sink to the bottom. You then pour off the excess water and allow the pigment to dry out. Afterwards it can be stored in a container for further use.

This method of application does work beautifully. Missing from the explanation is the recipe for the binder. Hilliard suggests adding sugar candy because it acts as a plasticizer and human ear wax because it slightly retards drying. However, judging how much sugar candy you could add while avoiding sparkle was a delicate matter. Both Hilliard and Norgate mention their distaste for any kind of shine from the paint and the addition of too much sugar candy causing sparkle, particularly in the blue background.

The next stage was to lightly block in features like hair and clothes.

The fashion for large, finely made ruffs offered artists a chance to show off the ability to portray complex lace patterns. The underlayer was usually blocked in a grey colour and the lace pattern produced by applications of thickened lead white paint. Hilliard used at least three different grades of white paint, each reserved for different effects.

Previously blocked in details and colours would be strengthened and finishing touches added before gems and inscriptions.

Gold and gems

A feature of some miniatures and a speciality of Hilliard is the depiction of gold and gems. Many of Hilliard's portraits have gold writing with flourishes. This was done with gold paint made from powdered gold and gum.

The depiction of gems in a hard, raised blob of translucent colour remains an enigma. Hilliard was rather secretive about this. It is generally thought that pigmented resin was applied as a translucent blob on a base of gold or silver leaf. It is also suggested that a heated metal tool can be used to do this; but this method does not leave a clean finish. Also, the resin takes a very long time to dry, which would render it vulnerable to dust. It is pertinent to remember that treatises giving information that could be used by other practitioners might not be quite accurate; after all, writers like Hilliard may well not have really wanted to give out trade secrets in a competitive market, and they may not have told the whole truth. According to Edward Norgate's interpretation of Hilliard:

To make Rubies delivered mee as a great secret in Cypher. In plaine English it is that on a ground of burnisht silver, of the fashion size of your Rubie, You take Turpentine of the best and Purest, temper it with Indian or Florence lake, then take a needle or such like small iron instrument. This must rest a day or two to dry and you will find it faire, and transparent. If it be long in drying, adde to it a little powder of clarified Masticke.

For an emerald, adde to Turpentaine, Verdigreece and a little Trumericke root scrapt, with Vineger. Let it dry, grind it into fine powder and temper it with Turpentine, as you did for the Rubie.

Nicholas Hilliard, *Queen Elizabeth I*, painted 1590–1603, body colour on vellum on a playing card, height 62 mm, width 47 mm Victoria and Albert Museum, London

A culinary failure of my own made me consider whether the jewels may have been made of sugar rather than resin. Sugar, mentioned as an ingredient for the binder, can be manipulated to be very hard. A hard, durable blob of sugar could have been created on a base colour of vermilion, madder, gold or silver. An experiment with very thick gum arabic and sugar produced a hard raised blob.

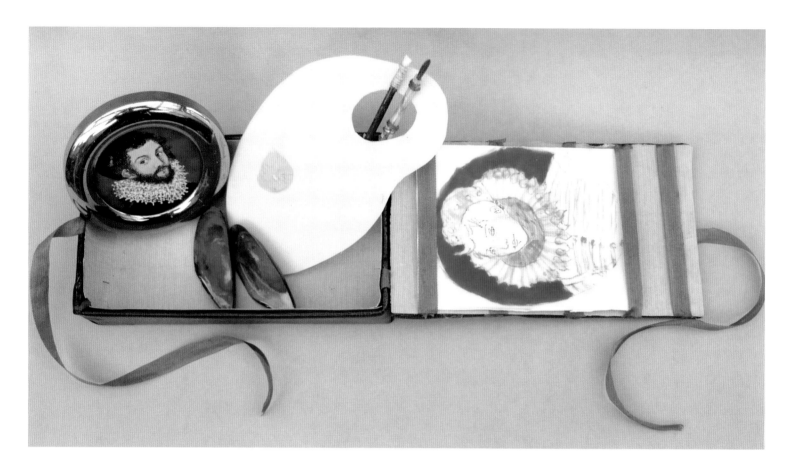

A pocket desk with shell palettes, small brushes, a burnisher made from a tiny tooth, a miniature in its early stages and a finished and framed miniature

Tools

As one might expect, the tools used for miniatures were all small. Brushes were made from the tail hairs of various small animals, including ermine, squirrel and stoat. The hairs were gathered together and shaped to a point, tied and pulled through a quill of a bird's feather that was then attached to a wooden or ivory stick. Contrary to popular belief, miniaturists did not favour brushes made of only a few hairs, as these are not good carriers of pigment. Such minimally haired brushes might be chosen for applying minute details like eyebrow hairs, but the most important quality for a brush is its ability to keep a point: so a brush with many hairs that taper to a fine point is most desirable. The flexibility of the hairs is also important. Palettes could be of ivory or shell: scallop or oyster.

Hilliard suggests having little tools for burnishing the gold paint and leaf: 'And with a pretty little tooth of some ferret or stoat or other wild little beast you may burnish your gold or silver here or there as need requireth.' My own burnisher, as before, was made from the pretty little tooth of one of my children.

Norgate describes a pocket desk he made for himself:

And because you should not be unfurnished with things necessary to take a picture from home as well as at home, be pleased to have in readiness such a box as I contrived for myselfe, of 6 inches long and 3 inches broad and 2 inches deepe that you may carry in your pocket the inside of your lid must be laid a cross with 4 penny or 6 penny greene Taffety ribbin, the whole length thereof begining at the hinges laying the ribbin a little one of the another, fastning the ribbin on the sides and covering the outsides with red leather, gilded if you please

After Hilliard

Over the next three centuries miniatures develop more in keeping with styles of larger paintings. Later miniatures were made on ivory supports rather than vellum.

Toward the end of his life Francisco de Goya (1746–1828) had a burst of working small. His miniatures were allegedly produced during his voluntary exile in Bordeaux. As an exile, Goya was looking for novel products that could generate income. Perhaps his interest in the genre was stimulated by his encouragement of Rosario, the daughter of his companion Leocadia Weiss. At the time painting in miniature was considered a reasonably respectable way of earning a living for a girl.

Goya was an innovator in all media; his approach to miniature painting was revolutionary. He used ivory as a support. Ivory was a difficult surface to work on with aqueous media,

Francisco de Goya, *Reclining Nude*, 1824–5, carbon black and watercolour on ivory, 87 × 86 mm
Museum of Fine Arts, Boston

Goya, *Man looking for fleas in his shirt*, 1824–5, carbon black and watercolour on ivory, 60 × 59 mm Museum of Fine Arts, Boston

and artists tried various techniques to get the paint to adhere to the not-so-porous support. It was suggested, for example, that it could be advantageous to add some ox gall (the bile of cattle!) to the water being used when mixing the paint, as its acidity would act as a degreaser. But Goya's way of working on ivory in miniature was very different from the way other artists had worked.

There is a description of how Goya worked by Antonia de Brugada, a young painter who assisted the aged Goya during the Bordeaux years.

His miniatures bore no resemblance to fine Italian miniatures nor even those of Jean Isabey . . . Goya had never been able to imitate anyone, and he was too old to begin. He blackened the ivory plaque and let fall on it a drop of water which removed part of the black ground as it spread out, tracing random light areas. Goya took advantage of these traces and always turned them into something original and unexpected. These little works were still in the vein of the Caprichos; today they would be very much sought after, if the dear man had not wiped off many of them in order to economize on the ivory. Those that remained at his death were, I believe, taken to Madrid by his son.

Brugada is describing here the way Goya would cover a small sheet of ivory in black watercolour paint (that is a pigment bound in gum arabic). He would then drop water on the painted surface and push it around randomly with brush or finger until the shapes that emerged suggested an image. He worked on this with brush and swab, adding and subtracting colours in layers and line, sometimes scratching. It is a very direct way of working compared with Hilliard's. Very few of Goya's miniatures survive, but those that do are intense little dramas produced in a 'stream of consciousness' way that seems unique to him.

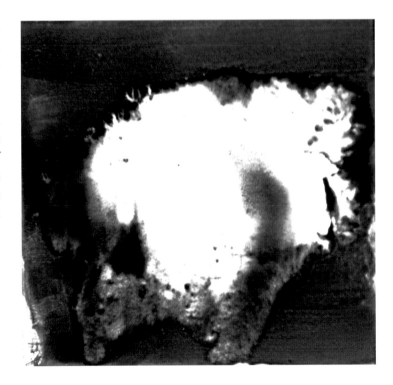

After Goya
Above A black blob of water-based paint dissolving into an idea for an image
Below left The image emerges. *Below right* Colour is added.

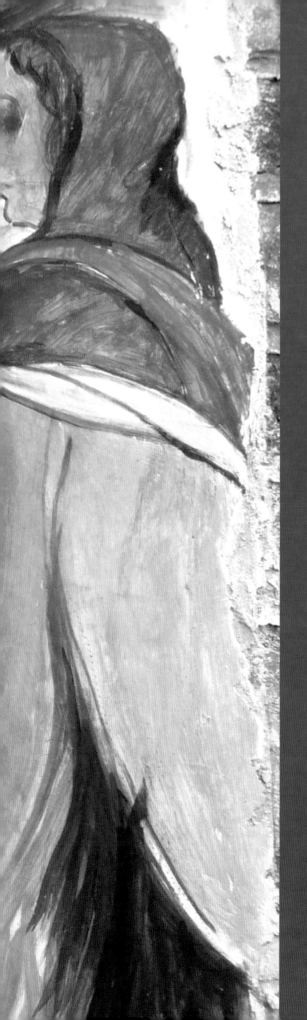

Fresco

Fresco

Feeding the hungry wall

Sister Lucia Wylie on creating fresco

Fresco is a permanent way of decorating walls and ceilings, indoors and, if the climate suits, outdoors too. Fresco developed from the more expensive technique of mosaic. Mosaic was applied to the same structural base as fresco, but the mosaic pieces were more expensive and took longer to apply than the paint layers of fresco. Fresco (from the Italian *fresco*, meaning 'fresh') is the application of colour to damp plaster before it sets. In true fresco (*buon fresco*) the pigment has no binder but is mixed only with water, and as it dries it becomes part of the wall. Very ancient examples survive from all over the world. In spite of natural disasters and war damage, Italy is particularly rich in surviving frescoes. The climate in Italy was fairly conducive to making fresco both inside and out, as long as the building was constructed to minimize moisture retention.

The decoration of walls in this way was used to tell stories and instruct. Centuries before universal education picture stories were a way of informing the illiterate. Frescoes are not private in the way that easel paintings or illuminated manuscripts are. They are mainly in public places, though some were rarely seen – for instance, those that were created for the private apartments of the Pope.

The golden age of fresco painting was between the late thirteenth century and the sixteenth century. Duccio (*c.* 1255–*c.*1318), Giotto (*c.* 1267–1337) and Lorenzetti (*c.* 1290–1348) made schemes in the pre-fifteenth-century technique of fresco described by Cennino in his *Libro dell'Arte*, while in the fifteenth and sixteenth centuries Leonardo, Titian (*c.* 1485–1576), Raphael (1483–1520) and Michelangelo worked in the way described by Giorgio Vasari in his *Lives of the Artists* (1550). Vasari was a contemporary of Michelangelo and a great admirer of his achievements. There was a resurgence of interest in fresco in the first half of the twentieth century.

Before embarking on fresco an artist needed to have a knowledge of the correct sequence of layers of wall construction and its finishing layers, if the fresco was to succeed. He also needed to understand how all the materials would react with each other and the local climate conditions. The complex chemical reactions between the base material, the mortar, the upper plaster layers and the pigment need to develop in the right way. Failure of any of the layers can cause permanent problems. Leonardo's *Last Supper* was doomed from the outset because there was no damp course in the refectory building where it was made. Centuries of restoration attempts – the most recent, in the twentieth century, taking twenty years – cannot bring back what has been permanently lost, but the recent work attempted to undo crude restorations of the past and forestall further damage. Damp is the enemy of fresco.

Understanding the appetite of the wall

The wall on which a fresco is made is like a body. The foundations – timber frame, wood, rubble – are the skeleton. On to this mortar, the flesh, is applied: first the *trussilatio* or scratch coat, and then the *arriccio*. This is followed by the *intonaco*, a much finer layer, like skin, on which the pigment is applied; as it dries it becomes one with the wall.

Giotto di Bondone, *The Marriage at Cana* (detail), *c.* 1305, fresco
Scrovegni (Arena) Chapel, Padua

Fresco is the most physically demanding of painting techniques and requires careful planning. The wall needs to be cleaned and saturated with water before the trussilatio – a rough mortar of approximately three parts coarse sand and one part slaked lime – is trowelled on. The arriccio that follows is a thinner layer, richer in lime – two parts sand to one part slaked lime. The final layer, the intonaco, is one part sand and possibly marble dust to one part mature slaked lime. The older the slaked lime the smoother and whiter it is.

Slaked lime is developed by extracting limestone from a quarry, roasting it in a kiln to drive off the water and then 'slaking' it in water. This is done by pouring water on the kiln-roasted lime. It bubbles vigorously before settling down to absorb water for a period of a few months, or longer – it is not unusual to store lime in water for two years. This preparation has to be done in carefully controlled conditions, as the lime is caustic (in times of plague it was sprinkled on the dead in pits to dissolve the bodies). The slaked lime becomes lime putty (also known as lime plaster). It can be diluted with water to produce limewash but for the intonaco it is spread on to the arriccio when it is thicker, say the consistency of butter. The slaked lime I used in my attempts at fresco came from a quarry in Derbyshire. There is still demand for this product today for use in the restoration of old houses, as modern cement and plaster do not combine well with old structures and are likely to crack.

Right Sinopia for the fresco of *Hell* by the Master of the Triumph of Death
Museo dell Sinopie, Camposanto, Pisa
Far right Master of the Triumph of Death, *Hell*, 1360–70, fresco
Museo Camposanto Monumentale, Pisa

Creating a fresco

Transferring the image

Before the fifteenth century, when paper was not produced in large sheets or in great quantity, small drawings were interpreted by eye and copied on to the arriccio or mortar layer while it was still damp. This was done with an earth colour, usually a red/brown that originally came from the Turkish area of Sinope. Hence the colour was called sinopia — and the drawings took the same name. These sinopias are the most exciting survivals of the artist's creative process. Often they are sketchy and relaxed, evidence of the artist's first thoughts and planning.

The amazing thing for us to comprehend is what followed the sinopia. The artist would cover the drawing with the intonaco. While it was still damp the drawing was then re-created from memory and colour was added. Sinopias are so interesting to see as some of them show that the artist may have changed the design on top. This is such a different attitude from ours, so hard for us to understand: it makes the adage 'drawn from memory' very poignant. It is as if the original drawing served as a rehearsal for what followed, the artist working like an actor or a musician remembering music.

Creating a fresco

Right Applying the arriccio over the trussilatio
Below left The arriccio in position
Below right Applying the intonaco

A charcoal outline of an image is drawn on the arriccio.

The sinopia is applied over the charcoal and fixed in the damp mortar.

The intonaco is applied, covering up the sinopia.

The lost image is redrawn.

The underpainting is applied, here in green earth with umber shadow.

The flesh is painted in white and vermilion tints; more modelling is added with hatched burnt sienna and the hair is painted in yellow ochre.

Right The cartoon for my fresco, ready for incising or pricking

Below left The cartoon is pricked.
Below right Charcoal dust is rubbed through the perforations on to the intonaco.

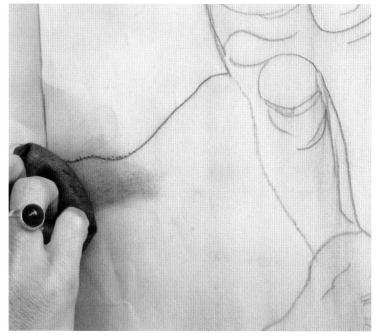

After the fifteenth century, when paper was produced in greater quantities, artists would transpose their ideas to the wall using a variety of paper transfer methods (see page 28). Sheets of paper were pasted together to create a large sheet and a drawing the same dimensions as the fresco was made. The lines of this were pricked and rubbed through with charcoal dust on to the damp plaster of the intonaco. Alternatively, the drawing was applied to the intonaco and a blunt stylus was used to incise the design. Evidence of the indents and the charcoal dots can be seen on some surviving frescoes.

Painting

Once the design was made the painting process began. True fresco (*buon fresco*) used only pigment and water which, when applied to the damp plaster, becomes one with the wall. This creates the greatest depth of colour. A more pastel look can be achieved by mixing dilute limewash with pigment.

Right The design transferred to the intonaco, showing the charcoal dots

The alternative method
Below left Incising the drawing on the intonaco
Below right The incised line on the intonaco

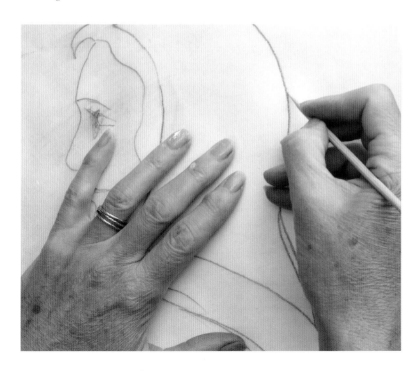

Above left Underpainting using earth red
(sinopia)

Above right My fresco of the prophet Jeremiah,
after Michelangelo

The artist needed to calculate the amount he could paint before the intonaco set. The temperature inside and outside would need to be considered each day. If a miscalculation was made and the day piece 'went off' the dry area could be cut away at an angle and the next day's intonaco carefully fitted to the angle in the way that would be least visible. The trick would be to have joins in discreet areas of the composition. These areas are visible in a raking light and give an insight into how much energy an artist would have had for a day.

Only certain colours were compatible with the lime in the plaster. Earth colours, like browns and yellows, combine really well, but mineral colours, especially ultramarine from lapis lazuli, need to be added *a secco* (that is, after the plaster has dried), using an egg or glue binder for the pigment. Sometimes this rule was not obeyed and there are some very dreary skies where the blue is fragmented or has largely fallen off, exposing the brown underpaint that was recommended under blue. Perhaps they thought the brown earth might protect mineral blue from the lime.

Secco

Vasari is scathing of *secco*. He more or less says that it is for cissies; for a real macho, bravura, risky performance only *buon fresco* will do. He sums up his attitude as follows:

> Of all the methods that painters employ, painting on the wall is the most masterly and beautiful, because it consists in doing in a single day that which, in the other methods, may be retouched day after day, over the work already done . . . fresco being truly the most manly, most certain, most resolute and durable of all the other methods, and as time goes on it continually acquires infinitely more beauty and harmony than do the others. Exposed to the air [it] throws off all impurities, water does not penetrate it, and it resists anything that would injure it. But beware of having to retouch it with colours that contain size prepared from parchment, or the yolk of egg, or gum, as many painters do, for besides preventing the wall from showing up the work in all clearness, the colours become clouded by that retouching and in a short time turn black. Therefore let those who desire to work on the wall work boldly in fresco and not retouch in the dry [secco] because, besides being a very poor thing in itself, it renders the life of the pictures short, as has been said in another place.

Vasari's *Lives of the Artists* culminates in a crescendo of praise for Michelangelo (they are said to have been good friends) and his Sistine Chapel work – the ultimate in tough-guy painting. Four years in the making, allegedly done by him alone up a scaffold, on his back, paint dripping down his arms, unable to step back and view progress for fear of falling off. In more recent times researchers have found that a lot of what Vasari said was myth: Michelangelo did not work alone – he had teams of assistants at different times – and the scaffold that was built made it unnecessary to work on his back. But he would have had to lean back at times, which wouldn't have been too comfortable. However, Michelangelo did use secco, as did many artists of previous centuries. It was necessary if you wanted to use certain colours, such as ultramarine. What Vasari understood about secco, though, is that it does not always last, and some surviving frescoes can look quite strange where the colours painted in secco have come off or have been attacked by mould. The animal or vegetable binder used with the pigment in secco is much more vulnerable to climate change and to mould when applied to plaster.

Accounts of the making of the frescoes of the Sistine Chapel by Michelangelo, Raphael and Sodoma (1477–1549) are riveting. Michelangelo's fresco cycle is the best known. When he began what became a four-year project he was not experienced in fresco, regarding himself primarily as a sculptor, and he certainly needed help from more experienced assistants to carry out the early stages. At the same time he had trouble at home from his family and political intrigues to navigate; he also had to sustain enormous physical and mental strength to carry through such a huge project. Many letters from Michelangelo survive, mostly complaining about the difficulties involved.

Over the centuries the Sistine ceiling has required some conservation work. Thousands of people visiting the Chapel have the audacity to breathe and emit other unmentionable gases that, combined with smoke from candles, have contributed to the discoloration of the frescoes. In the 1980s a massive restoration was undertaken that

There is needed also a hand that is dexterous, resolute and rapid, but most of all a sound and perfect judgement; because while the wall is wet the colours show up in one fashion, and afterwards when dry they are no longer the same.
Giorgio Vasari,
The Lives of the Artists, 1550

Michelangelo, *The Creation of Adam* (detail),
1508–12, fresco
Sistine Chapel, Vatican

people are still arguing over. I do not wish to enter the fray. I witnessed the work when it was half-completed and the colours of the cleaned areas were revealed to be very bright. This was wonderfully shocking juxtaposed to the kippered untouched areas.

Moving frescoes

For centuries frescoes have been moved or painted over, a bit as we would have the decorators in today. Indeed, records from various institutions show that change in prevailing taste has robbed us of works by artists who are now considered important. Some frescoes have been moved because of problems with the underlying building structure, such as damp and mould, which have required radical treatment.

Florence has a vast number of frescoes whose survival has often been threatened by the frequent flooding of the river Arno. In the 1960s there was such serious flooding that fast action was needed to save many frescoes. This accelerated the development of ways of separating them from walls. Sinopia and intonaco were separated from older frescoes, while post-fifteenth-century ones mainly required removal of the intonaco only.

Double layers of canvas were pasted to the surface using a water-soluble glue and the layers were gently pulled away. This sounds so simple and so dangerous, but apparently sometimes many metres of fresco were removed in one piece. Once separated from the wall the frescoes were weighted down and flattened. They were then mounted on rigid supports or on canvases. The protective canvases on the front were removed and the paintings displayed where they are seen today. Such treatments are very controversial but in the case of the Florentine floods it was necessary to act promptly to save what they could or the frescoes might have been lost. There are some very fine sinopias on display in the Camposanto at Pisa.

Frescoes in the twentieth century

There was a great surge of interest in fresco in the first half of the twentieth century, particularly from the Mexican muralists Diego Rivera (1886–1957), David Siqueiros (1896–1974) and Jose Climente Orozco (1883–1949). They came from a long tradition of public art and during the1920s and 1930s produced many large schemes that combined folklore and contemporary politics. They had international reputations. Notoriously, Diego Rivera produced a mural for Nelson Rockefeller in New York. When it was pointed out to Rockefeller that one of the chaps in the mural was Lenin, he asked Rivera to remove him. When he refused he was sacked, and the mural was destroyed. Luckily, Rivera had kept the designs and he produced another version that can today be seen at the Palacio de Bellas Artes in Mexico City.

The modern Mexican muralists at first tried to use what they thought was a more indigenous method of painting: encaustic. Pigment is bound in wax and resin, it is applied warm and liquid and then it is set into the surface by ironing over it to seal the paint. A story, probably apocryphal, about one of the Mexican artists says that he didn't see why they should use the methods of Cennino Cennini when Cennino had not been to Mexico — unlikely in the fourteenth century. However, the Mexican artists soon found encaustic too inconvenient and learned to use buon fresco instead.

So these artists used the same five-hundred-year-old techniques as dictated by Cennino, and trained a lot of young artists to use them, including Diego Rivera's wife, Frida Kahlo (1907–1954), who had first seen Rivera when he was producing a mural at her school. David Siqueiros eventually adopted acrylic paint for murals.

In America the influence of the Mexican muralists increased during the 1930s, when public art was given a boost by the short-lived but inspired New Deal scheme initiated by President Franklin Roosevelt, by which the state funded artists in the visual arts and theatre to work on community art projects.

The experience of doing fresco is rather romantically explained in the writings of an American nun, Sister Lucia Wylie (1906–1998), who painted many frescoes long before she saw any by the Italian artists of the Renaissance that she admired. In fact she didn't

Above and below Photographs taken in Florence in the 1960s, showing layers of fresco being removed from a wall

Diego Rivera, *Man, Controller of the Universe*
(detail), 1934, fresco
Museo del Palacio de Bellas Artes, Mexico City

even see a colour reproduction until she was over thirty. Nevertheless, she developed a passion for the process. Below are extracts from her descriptions of how she worked.

One of the most stimulating things about fresco painting is that the plaster has a life of its own, with its own needs and appetite for water, paint, and various brush pressures.

Then, about midnight, the plaster says, 'sorry, no more'. If you try to force it to take more paint and water, it actually almost spits it back at you. The day's painting is over whether or not you feel the work is right. Twenty or more hours of the maintaining of constant recollection is behind you, and all of you aches with weariness; yet all of you is joyful over having been given another fresco day.

The day's painting is then over — twenty-two hours at a northern latitude, further south twelve or fourteen or sixteen hours before crystallization begins to set in. Sometime before, nearer the middle of the day, the leftover edge was carefully trimmed away. Any unpainted or unfinished parts are now trimmed out down to the plaster coat underneath to await another day similar to this one. Since it was my technique to lay each piece of plaster larger than I intended to paint so that the surrounding areas held the moisture longer, the trimming process in my work took a little longer than usual.

Finally tomorrow's section is marked off on the wall and is given a good soaking with water. Each day the drama is re-enacted — piece by piece, day by day, as the painting grows toward completion.

The day's stretch of twenty hours of hard physical labour, of constant creative awareness, is over — and more twenty-hour days are just ahead. How can one continue to paint these twenty-hour stretches? I have found I can do it by working on a forty-eight-hour day. But this sounds even worse — perhaps I will have to tell you how it is done.

This strange day begins about noon, when I get up and go to the job — cleaning up brushes and paints from the day before, and getting all in readiness for the painting session. This takes until dinnertime, followed by an early bedtime. 3:30 in the morning comes early and at 4 the plasterer and myself are on the job, beginning this twenty-hour stretch. Meals are eaten on the scaffold. I have often wondered who took Michelangelo his meals — up there so high on the scaffold in the Sistine Chapel; it wouldn't have been so bad for Fra Angelico — he had a corps of Brothers to wait on him, but Michelangelo worked alone.

One may take the comment about Michelangelo with a pinch of salt — the Pope's great artist probably did get fed!

My own brief experience of fresco for this book has increased my awe for those who could stand working in difficult, often wet and cold conditions for hours, days and months; coordinating all the different skills that go into making a fresco — including the small matter of designing a brilliant scheme. It is definitely a team activity: you need a skilled plasterer, someone to mix the paint and hand it to you, someone to wash the brushes and someone to keep you fed and watered during long days of work. The artists of the early and high Renaissance also needed a head for heights and a trust in the person who built the scaffold. It is perhaps worth mentioning that whether working high up or on the ground it is important to work top down, or there is a risk of dripping paint on the work, on yourself or on passers-by. Just a couple of *giornate* (day pieces) absolutely exhausted me, but I am looking forward to doing more: it is a magical process.

Egg tempera

Egg tempera

Egg tempera is the name given to the medium created by mixing pigment with egg yolks and water. The idea of painting with egg may seem bizarre, but the combination of egg and water makes a quick-drying paint, and egg, separated or whole, was used in various techniques, including manuscript illumination, miniatures and fresco. In fact before the increased use of slow-drying oil, egg yolk was the most frequently used binder for paint. The technique of painting with egg tempera (the word tempera comes from the Latin verb *temperare*, to mix), was used by the ancient Egyptians and the Romans, reaching a peak of sophistication in the early Renaissance in the work of artists like Duccio, Fra Angelico (*c.* 1395–1455), Piero della Francesca (*c.* 1412–1492) and Botticelli (1445–1510).

Technically egg tempera has two things in common with fresco: the speed of drying and the fact that the ground layer is an absorbent plaster of either gypsum or chalk bound with animal-skin glue. It differs from fresco in that the plaster is worked on when dry and not damp. Most painting in egg tempera is on wood panels. In Italy the wood most commonly used was poplar, not because it is the best but because it was plentiful. Poplar has large 'pores' and tends to be more moisture-retentive than superior, close-grained cedar wood. Cedar was reserved for structural work in buldings, ships and furniture. Northern European artists favoured panels made of oak. Whichever wood was used, the construction of a panel was a special skill, and the job would be done by a cabinet- or panel-maker. Only the quarter-sawn section of a tree was really suitable because it had the straightest grain and was therefore less likely to warp. Because there was a limited amount of this wood from each tree, panels were, of necessity, composed from several pieces. The larger the picture scheme the more pieces of wood with joins that needed to be concealed.

Some panel paintings would be just one plain flat surface but others would perhaps make up a complex altarpiece with a main picture, some wings, and possibly predellas. Predellas are a sequence of little pictures attached to the periphery of the main one, but they are none the less important adjuncts, often telling a story (rather like a comic strip). Sadly, many altarpieces from the Renaissance have been dismantled and bits are found in museums all over the world. This separation makes a nonsense of the overall concept of the artist. Additionally, all this may be contained in elaborately carved and gilded frames that are part of the same structure.

The process

Preparing the panel
To conceal the joins and the grain of the wood to create a perfect surface on which to apply egg tempera, a considerable ground layer was required. Cennino is a good guide to the process, explaining the sequence, the materials and even the required weather conditions.

He recommends planing the flats of wood that have been joined together and then applying a couple of layers of glue size, the first one weaker than the second.

. . . and you know what the first size with water accomplishes? Not being so strong, it is just as if you were fasting, and ate a handful of sweetmeats, and drank a glass of

Sandro Botticelli, *Birth of Venus* (detail), *c.* 1485, egg tempera on canvas
Uffizi Gallery, Florence

Piero della Francesca, *The Baptism of Christ*, 1450s, egg tempera on poplar, 1670 × 1160 mm National Gallery, London

good wine, which is an inducement for you to eat your dinner. So it is with this size: it is a means of giving the wood a taste for receiving the coats of size and gesso.

The glue used throughout the process of preparing the panel goes by the name of animal-skin or rabbit-skin glue. This is really a general name for glue made by rendering different bits of animals: skin, hoofs, snouts, ears and tails. It could also be made from offcuts of other processes like leather-tanning or parchment-making. Preferably all should come from the same batch, as each batch could be a different strength and that could have an effect on the bond.

Cennino goes on to advise that once the coats of size have been applied the surface should be covered with thin, grease-free linen cloth that has been dipped in glue. This is to cover the joins, to prevent any branch notches from moving and to serve as a tooth for the gesso that follows.

Cennino recommends two kinds of gesso: *grosso* and *sottile*. The grosso is heavier and rougher than the sottile and was used as a base layer prior to the finer sottile. Less complex flat panel structures needed only the gesso sottile. Gesso sottile is the same gypsum as the grosso but it is refined by slaking in water for a month and then dried in little cakes. The cakes are then chopped into a casserole and animal-skin glue is poured over. The mixture is heated and gently stirred until it is, in Cennino's words, 'as if you are making batter for pancakes'. It should never be allowed to become hotter than blood. It must not boil.

The first coat can be rubbed into the surface with the palm of the hand, then approximately seven more coats are brushed on; each one must be just damp to the touch before the next one is applied. The aim is to create a smooth, white surface with no brushmarks. Each layer becomes one with its predecessor, and the whole should eventually be three or more millimetres in thickness. All the layers need to be applied before the day is over, regardless of the size of the panel, and the mixture must be from one batch. So, as with fresco, understanding what you can achieve before the materials set is an important knack.

Weatherwise, Cennino says: 'and know that this sizing and gessoing call for dry and windy weather. Size wants to be stronger in summer than in winter.'

Once the gesso has been dry for about two days the final treatment of the surface prior to painting is to rub charcoal over the surface and then scrape it smooth. You know that it is smooth when the charcoal doesn't show. It is a cruel and time-consuming process but worth it in the end, as eventually Cennino says it will 'come out like ivory'. He also says that the resulting charcoal/gesso dust is useful for rubbing on vellum or parchment to take out oiliness (by which perhaps he means greasy fingermarks).

Drawing up

The surface is now ready for the drawing up. A full-sized cartoon (see page 28) was sometimes used; or, as Cennino suggests, the composition could be worked out lightly in charcoal attached to a stick (to get a distance from the work) and then fixed with quill and ink. Feathers were used for sweeping away excess charcoal and erasing changes or mistakes.

Infra-red photography has revealed how detailed these underdrawings were, and it is understandable that having made such careful preparation of the panel you would also

Duccio di Buoninsegna, *The Virgin and Child with
Saints Dominic and Aurea, c.* 1315, egg tempera on
poplar, centre panel 610 × 390 mm
National Gallery, London

carefully prepare and plan the painting. For artists of the fourteenth and fifteenth centuries the careful planning might include some flashy perspective – for example, architectural structures receding from the picture plane. This was an evolving science, mathematically calculated to pull the viewer into the scene. Infra-red photography not only reveals elaborate underdrawing if it is present, but can also show incised lines on the gesso ground, which may have been done with a silverpoint stylus.

Gold work

In the thirteenth and fourteenth centuries it was common for altarpieces to have a gold background that glowed in the candle-lit church, creating mystery, reflecting light and denying space. There might also be gold in various areas of the painting – perhaps for a saint's halo, or to decorate a robe. Any gold work would be applied before the rest of the painting. The area to be covered was painted with a layer of red clay or bole. Breathing on the bole drew its glue binder to the surface. Then the gold leaf was cut and lifted with a brush and moved to the surface, where it would be sucked on to the bole, attracted by the moisture. When it was dry it was burnished – usually with a smoothed stone, perhaps an agate – to a mirror-like shine. Artists achieved fantastically decorative effects by punching gold with designs, using a variety of stamping and incising tools. They were not supposed to pierce the gold (as I couldn't avoid doing in my attempts shown here). Other extravagant effects were achieved by applying paint over gold and then gently scraping away the paint to create a gold pattern; this was called *sgraffito*.

Applying the paint

The range of pigments compatible with egg tempera on gesso was wider than with fresco. The gesso surface was slightly absorbent, and that could be used to advantage; alternatively, the absorbency could be reduced by applying a layer of animal-skin glue to the surface before beginning to paint.

Contrary to what might be expected, the egg yolk has little effect on the colour, and over time the colours remain brighter than those bound in oil, which can change in as little as twenty-five years because of the yellowing of the oil and any added resin.

The effects achieved with this fast-drying medium were carefully worked out and controlled. If egg tempera is applied with bold, sweeping strokes, to form a continuous film of paint, there is a danger that it will dry too quickly and flake off. So, instead, artists used tiny, short brushstrokes, building them up in layers. These strokes linked to form a strong bond with the gesso.

Finally the decorative parts of the painting were added. These were often made with gold in different techniques, using gold leaf and shell gold.

Above, from left to right Design drawn on gesso ground; red bole on areas to be gilded; verdaccio, the underpaint for flesh colour; pink strokes, the beginning of the build-up of skin colour

Below Various forms of gold decoration: stamped designs in gold haloes; sgraffito patterns in vermilion over gold; patterns painted in shell gold on the border of the ultramarine robe

Above left Applying the gesso
Above right Drawing up

Artists' training

Before the setting up of academies in the eighteenth century, and schools of art in the nineteenth, the training of artists mainly went on in workshops run by artists, who were in turn controlled by guilds that were run as tightly as trade unions. The guilds dictated the length of time an artist was apprenticed and what techniques he would be trained to use. With the aim of protecting the native artists, the guilds also operated restrictive practices, trying to restrict foreign workers and imports – not just people from other countries but also people from other parts of the same country. It was hard for incomers to penetrate this closed shop, but some foreign artists did, either because they had such a reputation that their services were much desired and the rules were flouted, or because they were devious enough to bend the rules. Perhaps, too, exceptions might be made if there were new ways of working to be learned from the foreigner.

Reconstructing a fifteenth-century panel

When I was asked to make a reconstruction of *The Madonna Adoring the Infant Christ* by Andrea del Verrocchio (*c.* 1435–1488), the experience taught me a great deal about painting practice in Florence in the fifteenth century, and greatly increased my admiration for the Florentine artists' skills.

Ruskin bought this painting, commonly known as the Ruskin Madonna, in 1875, for the museum he had established in Sheffield, and during the following century it was on public display there. However, in 1975 it was sold to the National Gallery of Scotland in Edinburgh, where it now hangs. *The Madonna* has suffered greatly over the centuries. Not only have the colours naturally aged — some have darkened, others faded — but as part of a Victorian 'restoration' the painting was transferred from a worm-eaten and fragile panel to a canvas. It must have been considered essential to do this, as it is a very radical treatment, dangerous to the painting. It involves protecting the front of the painting with special paper and paste and shaving the wood from the back right down to the paint layer. Along the way a third of the original paint was lost. The remaining paint was cleaned; then over the following century darkened varnish concealed what was left. Nearly a third of what can be seen now is not by Verrocchio or his pupils but by its most recent conservator, the late John Brearley, who restored it in 1974. His retouchings cleverly match the state of what remains. He could not possibly have used the original colours without unbalancing the picture entirely.

But I had none of his constraints. My brief was to produce, not a copy of the picture in its present state, but a reconstruction of what it might have looked like when it left Verrocchio's studio. I had to experiment with painting methods, but not on such a large scale. I used Cennino and other books as my guide, since, unlike the artists of fifteenth-century Florence, I had not been trained in these techniques since childhood. To them, many of the processes, especially the tiny hatching brushstrokes used for egg tempera, would have been easy.

Preparatory work

At the National Gallery of Scotland I examined the original painting and obtained pigment samples. Of particular importance were the cross-sections of samples taken from the Madonna's robe and its lining. The blue colour is azurite and the lining, which appears dark brown, was confirmed as malachite green, probably with a malachite glaze. X-rays of the picture (discovered at the Courtauld Institute after they had been lost for thirty-five years) also helped, particularly in reconstructing the perspective. The x-rays were easy to read because the lines were probably drawn with a lead or silver stylus, which leaves a pencil-like mark and an incision. The left-hand arch of the ruined temple is so carefully drawn that it might suggest a different and more accomplished hand than the one that painted the upper layer. It is difficult to avoid the thought that this part of the drawing could be by Verrocchio's most gifted pupil, Leonardo, but this is speculation.

Below An x-ray of the arch of the ruined temple on the left of the painting
Bottom My reconstruction of the arch

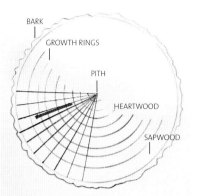

A section of a tree, quarter-sawn to ensure non-warping

Making the panel. Here the cabinet-maker is cutting a butterfly joint.

The panel

A cabinet-maker, Barnabas Trott, constructed a facsimile of a fifteenth-century panel from seasoned poplar. Then I sized the panel on both sides with animal-skin glue, attached a fine linen cloth to the face, and painted it with several coats of gesso. Foolishly, I failed to heed Cennino's advice to wait for 'dry and windy weather': I applied the gesso on a wet spring day in England – and discovered how right he was, when a whole host of cracks appeared the next day. Cennino doesn't tell how to remove the gesso, so I had to work that out for myself. The linen cloth layer that I had applied had not been trimmed and I wet a strip of the surface and then pulled hard, using the untrimmed fabric as a handle. This removed the gesso strip by strip in a rather satisfying way – like leg waxing! I waited for a dry day before successfully reapplying my gesso.

Practice pieces for the head of the Madonna

More practice pieces for the Madonna's
head, and one for the baby

The composition

The last conservator to work on the painting could only reconstruct areas of loss, some
of them fairly extensive, using the remaining paint as a guide. In my reconstruction, I was
freer to resolve problems of colour changes, paint loss and composition, exploring other
paintings of the period as source material. For example, in the Edinburgh picture the
baby has nothing to lean on; I have given him some fallen masonry padded by sheaves of
wheat. I have turned the right-hand side of the painting, where the area past the last

Practice pieces for the Madonna and
her robes

The drawing transferred from the cartoon
to the gesso ground

The Madonna's hands, showing
the underdrawing

Right Sprinkling charcoal dust through the perforations of the cartoon, to transfer the design for the embroidery on the edge of the Madonna's robe

Far right The gilded embroidery

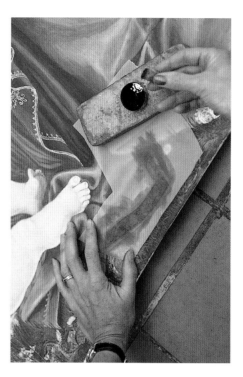

column is vague, into a broken wall, suggesting that there is a dark hollow behind it. The flora at the bottom of the original is obscured by pigment change or paint loss, but I was able to identify some of the plants. That nearest the baby is vervain, used as a salve for wounds. Supposed to have grown at the foot of the Cross, it prefigures Christ's death. The other plants are plantains, daisies, woodruff and wild strawberry. All have medicinal qualities except the strawberry, which represents the sweetness of the Virgin.

The floor was puzzling, as in the original painting there was a lack of continuity between the perspective on the left- and right-hand sides. Close scrutiny of the x-rays showed where the three members of the panel must once have been taken apart and put back together wrongly, throwing the whole perspective slightly out. I adjusted the drawing to correct the discrepancy.

Having worked on the composition, I made a full-sized cartoon and transferred it to the gessoed surface. I reinforced the drawing with ink and incised the perspective lines with silverpoint.

The painting

Following the order of painting recommended in treatises of the period, I started with buildings then moved on to clothes and flora before, finally, tackling the people. I used natural pigments; they were the best available, but their quality was very variable. I think they were probably inferior to Verrocchio's. I used egg yolk and water as a medium. There was no clear result from an analysis of the original medium, but close examination suggested that it was likely to have been egg tempera, although there may also have been some oil and resin. I used approximately eighty-five organic free-range eggs. Their quality varied from batch to batch, slightly affecting the tone of the colours. The variation

Far left Showing the green
earth underpainting for the
Madonna's flesh
Left Her glowing skin, after the
pink flesh colour has been
applied over the underpaint
Below The baby, leaning against
wheat-padded masonry

is perhaps attributable to differences in chicken feed. The haloes
and gold embroideries were done with an oil resin mordant and
gold leaf. The mordant is a sticky glue, the consistency of icing
from a fine nozzle, that is allowed to set until it is slightly tacky and
the gold leaf sticks to it. Most of the embroidery designs could be
taken from the pattern remaining on the original, but the pattern
for the robe lining came from other paintings of the period.

I used azurite blue, vermilion red, carmine red from cochineal,
raw umber, terre verte, malachite, verdigris, yellow ochre, flake
white, ivory black, and gold.

Equal amounts of egg yolk to pigment plus a little water is the
general rule. But some colours require different amounts of
grinding, and of binder. The artist needed to assess the quality and
individual character of each batch of natural pigment. Gradations
of colour were worked out carefully in advance of painting a
particular area. The colours could be ground in water in
reasonable quantities, but the egg tempera would only be added
just as the painting was to commence. Only small amounts could
be mixed at a time because it would dry out and become

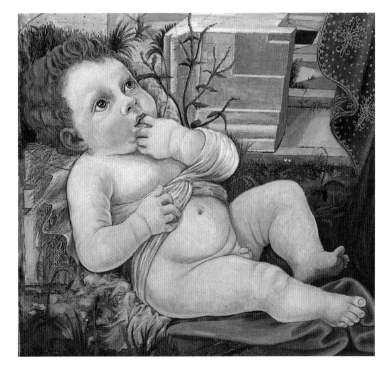

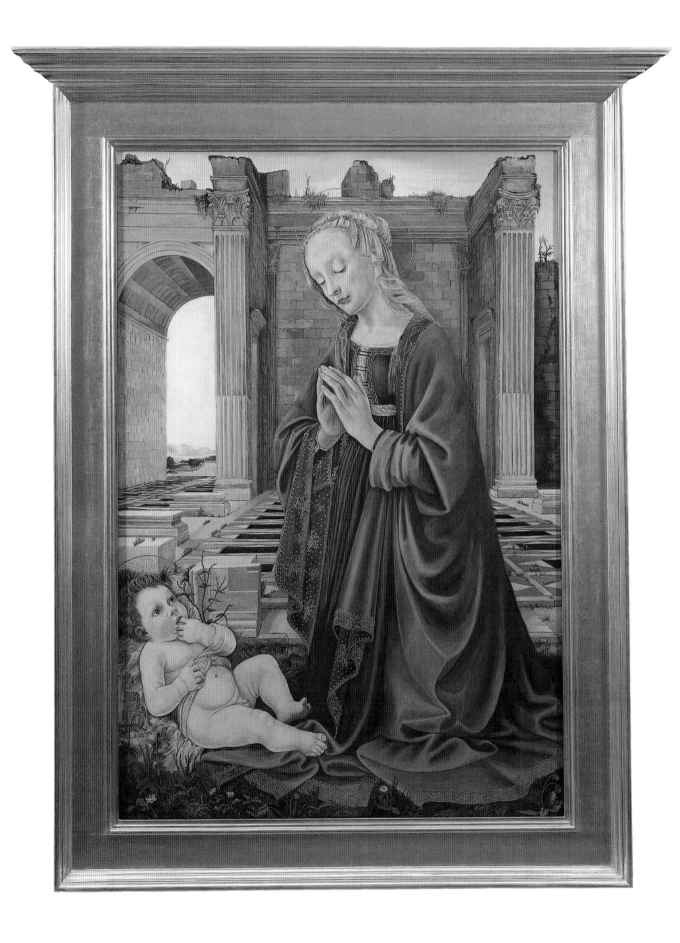

Reconstruction as an alternative to restoration

I think it is worth mentioning the difference between restoration and conservation. To restore is to bring back and to conserve is to arrest further deterioration. If you don't know how something really looked you cannot restore it. Conservation cannot bring back what is lost. Reconstruction is a useful and harmless speculation to show how an artwork may have looked. Digital technology creating virtual reconstruction is no substitute for real materials to get the look and feel of how something may have been. There are a number of paintings that really cannot be touched without an international furore, and many paintings are in an awful state. You cannot turn back time. For instance, the colours of the Mona Lisa are changed and obscured by a discoloured varnish. Wouldn't it be interesting to make several reconstructions to show how it might have looked?

Above Andrea del Verrocchio, *The Madonna Adoring the Infant Christ, c.* 1470, egg tempera and oil on canvas, transferred from panel, 1067 × 763 mm
National Gallery of Scotland, Edinburgh
Opposite My reconstruction of the Verrocchio panel

unworkable within about half an hour. This was really important when working with the more expensive pigments, such as ultramarine.

Draperies were painted using three tones, going from dark to light. For instance, if it was a Madonna's blue robe, the blue was applied first then white was added to make gradations of lighter and lighter blue working up toward a highlight on a fold. My Madonna's robe was identified as azurite. This was a relief: it was expensive, at £25 for 10 grams, but at least it wasn't ultramarine, as lapis lazuli would have cost twice that.

To paint flesh, Cennino recommends the use of an underlayer of green earth mixed with white lead. Green earth is a mineral, celadonite, found in Italy around Verona and Venice. There are also deposits in Cyprus. In a number of surviving pre-1400 paintings, the upper layer of the flesh paint has worn away, leaving an eerie green and pink skin; the Madonna is often distinctly nauseous-looking. After the green underpaint the verdaccio was added to model the form. This was a mix of colours to create one shadowing colour. The figure would at this point have looked like a metal sculpture. The artist worked in short hatched strokes, building up a network of almost 'knitted' colour gradations. Cennino recommends that the three tones of pinkish flesh colour be applied over the form to allow tiny amounts of the green to show through. The green and the pink are complementary and the eye mixes it into a rather wonderful glowing skin. In my example I followed Cennino's method and it gives a good idea of how a freshly painted face would have looked.

Finishing

I chose clarified egg white for the final coating, as it gives a dull satin finish that may also enrich the medium. Treatises of the time suggest this as a temporary coating until the egg is completely set.

*Leonardo! Strange diseases
strike at madders mixed with lead:
nun-pale now are Mona Lisa's
lips that you had made so red.*
Vladimir Nabokov, *Pnin,* 1956

Oil painting

Oil painting

Pigment combined with oil made it possible for artists to tell a story, make a portrait or a still life that looked so convincing that it could be mistaken for reality – real plants, fabrics, jewels, skin, fur and precious metals portrayed in paint. Jan van Eyck in the fifteenth century and Holbein in the sixteenth are fine exemplars of oil painting. The artist tells the viewer: 'This is how it looks, I want you to know this.' Holbein's portraits practically breathe. We can read so much about the people in his pictures. He portrays clothes as though he understands how they were made, embroideries as though he could have made the stitches – he paints them as though he is sewing them. Oil paint made it possible for artists to convey to the viewer ideas and reality on a flat surface. Jan van Eyck tells us that he was there, a witness, as he and his signature are glimpsed in the mirror of 'The Arnolfini Marriage' portrait. Although we are separated by hundreds of years from the people in Holbein's portraits, he can make us believe the sitter is communicating with both him and us.

This sort of bringing to life was not so convincing with aqueous media because the colours dried too quickly to be smoothly blended. Painting in egg tempera or fresco could make you believe but it could not fool you into picking a fly off a flower, as people have been said to do with a Dutch oil painting of the eighteenth century.

The use of oil as a binding medium for pigment did not just suddenly happen. Artists had used different drying oils for centuries. A drying oil is a vegetable oil that dries to a tough film, not by evaporation but by changing from a liquid to a solid compound. The oils most used are linseed from the flax plant, walnut and poppy. Vasari credits the increased popularity in the use of drying oils in Italy to developments in northern Europe. He mentions the Flemish artists Van Eyck (*c.* 1395–1441) and Rogier van der Weyden (1399–1464) and the Italian Antonella da Messina (*c.* 1429–1479) as great exponents of working on panel and canvas with oil paint. Vasari suggests that Antonello learned from Flemish artists on his travels and taught others in Italy to use the medium in the new way, but this is speculation.

Vasari praises the way that oil paint dries slowly, allowing for alterations and the blending of colours that when done skilfully makes the image 'seem to us in relief and ready to issue forth from the panel.'

Jan van Huysum, *Vase with Flowers*,
c. 1720, oil on panel, 791 × 606 mm
Dulwich Picture Gallery, London

Jan van Eyck, *The Portrait of Giovanni Arnolfini and his Wife* ('The Arnolfini Marriage'), 1434, oil on oak, 822 × 600 mm
National Gallery, London

Realism in northern Europe

The slow drying process means that oil paint can continue to be manipulated while it is still wet, so tones can be blended seamlessly. Oil paint takes much longer to dry than water-based media – weeks or months, depending on the type of oil. Artists were freed from the little hatched strokes of egg tempera; they could smooth and blend the paint with large strokes of the brush. Northern European artists of the fourteenth and fifteenth centuries aimed for a brushmark-free and lifelike effect.

Hans Holbein the Younger, *Jean de Dinteville and*
Georges de Selve ('The Ambassadors'), 1533,
oil on oak, 2070 × 2095 mm
National Gallery, London

Caravaggio, *Death of the Virgin*, c. 1606,
oil on canvas, 3690 × 2450 mm
Louvre, Paris

The drama of the south

In southern Europe in the sixteenth and seventeenth centuries painters in oil produced work with dramatic contrast of dark and light. Their painting was not so much striving after reality as expressing drama. The use of darker ground layers and backgrounds became popular with these southern artists. One could almost say that the further south the artist was working the darker their ground layer. This was not universally true, but Tintoretto (1518–1594) in Venice, Caravaggio (1571–1610), who worked his way from Rome down to the bottom of Italy and over to Malta, and Murillo (1618–1682) in Spain were all artists who used dark grounds. Tintoretto and Caravaggio in particular did massive, busy pictures. Tintoretto's *Crucifixion* in the Scuola Grande di San Rocco in Venice (see page 105) and Caravaggio's *Death of the Virgin* in the Louvre are examples of the dark background being used to create cavernous, mysterious depth. Perhaps we should also take into account the fact that both artists were in a hurry to produce large works: the dark background speeds up the painting process, because dark paint creates depth without the need to fill in too many details. The viewer is drawn into the void.

Preparation

The preparation of wooden panels remained pretty much the same as for tempera (see pages 78–81), except that examination of fourteenth- and fifteenth-century panels shows that there was less use of two kinds of gesso. The many layers that Cennino recommends were reduced; indeed some panels were barely coated with gesso and many do not have the thin linen layer covering the whole area of the panel. It was important to make the gesso less absorbent and this was achieved by rubbing oil into it. It was desirable sometimes to reduce the brightness of the gesso by applying a tinted ground layer. The tint was rarely a strong colour but could be beige or grey; it was composed of size and pigment or oil and pigment.

Canvas was quite a different matter. The fabric was not made specifically for artists' use but for more practical applications like mattress covers and sails for boats. However, from antiquity canvas had also been used for temporary paintings like banners, and backdrops for pageants and parties. The advantages of painting on canvas were that it was lightweight and could be rolled for easy transportation. It became especially popular in Venice in the sixteenth century because wooden panels were susceptible to woodworm and moulds induced by the damp climate. The disadvantages of canvas were that it could be torn or dented, or become slack on its stretcher.

The fabrics used were woven from hemp or flax threads. The fineness or coarseness of the weave was variable, as was its pattern: it could be tabby, herringbone, and sometimes damask. Damask, a textile with a woven pattern (white damask linen table cloths spring to mind), was a strange choice. Damask linen would not have added strength to the canvas but perhaps it contributed unseen luxury. We don't really know why it was used, but examples of its use have been found in some large paintings by Murillo of religious subjects; perhaps – as a person who was said to be devout – he thought it conveyed extra respect for the subject.

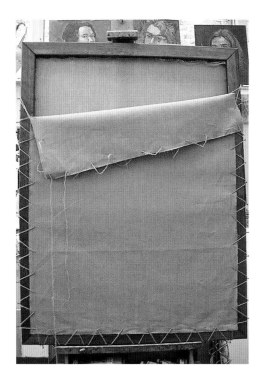

Stretching a canvas by stringing

Canvas was woven to less than a metre in width, so for a large painting pieces of fabric had to be sewn together. Instructions for sewing canvases make a virtue of the stitches being invisible. Today, though, the seams are sometimes apparent, as over time they have been pressed through to the front of the painting by linings that have been applied to the backs of the canvas to strengthen them as they have become fragile with age.

Stretching the canvas

The preparation of the canvas involved stretching on a wooden frame to make it as taut as possible. Sometimes this was done on a temporary stretcher: the canvas was tacked on but not turned over the edge of the stretcher; or it could be strung on the edge of the stretcher by inserting cord or string through the edges of the canvas and looping it over nails around the edge of the stretcher; the cord was then pulled around the nails to create an even tension. This allowed the sizing and ground layers to be applied all the way to the edge. Also, if the artist decided to enlarge or reduce the dimensions of the picture the canvas could be adjusted accordingly. Sometimes a black border was painted round the edge of the composition to accommodate tack or string holes and this area could also accommodate the weave distortion that could result from stretching. The finished painting would then either be put on a more permanent stretcher with its edges turned over, or stuck on a panel, or have panels inserted within the back of the stretcher.

Sizing the canvas

Once the canvas was stretched, it was sized, usually with glue. As the glue dried, the canvas became taut. The size coat also prevented the oil from penetrating to the back of the canvas. The glue was made from parchment clippings or glovemakers' remaindered fine skins, or from 'the inedible parts of animals', as Francisco Pacheco (father-in-law of Velasquez) put it in his treatise *L'Arte de la Pintura*. Skin and 'parts' were rendered and allowed to set to a jelly. Pacheco was quite specific about some of these parts: for instance, he said that sheep's ears make particularly fine gelatinous glue. The glue needed to be jellied so that its strength could be judged before being reliquidized by heating. The strength of the glue was adjusted by diluting it with water and the glue was used for a variety of tasks.

Priming the canvas

Primings fill the interstices (the hollows of the weave) to control the absorbency of the paint. Artists used many different recipes, to meet many different needs. Here is a selection from Pacheco. He is vague about quantities.

- Gacha, a mix of flour, mill dust, oil and honey cooked together: 'you could almost eat this even without appetite.' Spread over stretched canvas to fill the weave. When dry rub with pumice.
- Gesso made with size. Spread thinly over the canvas. Rub with pumice when dry.
- Size and sifted ashes.
- Clay from Seville, with the addition of white lead, red lead and charcoal bound in linseed oil. This was his preferred recipe. It would have made a warm brown priming.

Adam Elsheimer, *St Lawrence Preparing for Martyrdom*, c. 1600, oil on copper, 268 × 208 mm National Gallery, London

Painting on copper

Other surfaces, including stone, slate, plastered walls and metals, were also used for oil painting. Copper was particularly popular for small paintings in the seventeenth century. The reason for this was linked to developments in engraving and etching in the fifteenth century, along with the first printing presses. Engraving and etching made possible the duplication of images. For engraving, the lines were cut into a metal (usually copper) plate. For etching, the lines were drawn on the plate through a smoked black wax ground layer and then the lines were 'bitten' in an acid bath. Either method could be used to create a print by inking the plate, wiping off the excess so that ink remained only in the incised or acid-bitten lines, placing paper on the plate and putting it through a printing press. A plate was used repeatedly until the lines printed were faint or the artist decided that no more prints should be made from that plate. Some artists would use the backs or even the fronts of used plates as a surface for oil paint. Convenient or economical? But not all paintings on copper are on used plates.

Perhaps the vogue for painting on copper was inspired by the process of enamelling on copper, by which powdered colours, many from ground glass or minerals, are applied to copper plates and cooked on to them in a very hot kiln. The colours become liquid in the heat and set when cooled; the result is a shiny, glazed picture or design fused to the metal. Oil painting on copper can achieve a similar effect without the complexities and risk of technical failure of the enamelling process.

Paintings on copper tended to be small and therefore portable; they were also durable. The small size may be due to the technical difficulty of making large sheets of copper. However, sometimes several small paintings on copper were assembled to make a large narrative piece.

Why choose copper? Perhaps because you wanted to work on a smooth surface. It is conducive to a brushmark-free effect, to looking untouched by hand. An artist might also like to use the reflective quality of the pinky copper as an integral part of the design, or enjoy the lack of the weave texture of canvas. Copper was also lightweight and thin, and not susceptible to mould, dents, tears or woodworm.

Using a feather to smooth paint on a
copper surface

Three stages of preparation prior to
painting: dots, line, shading

Undercolour

Prepararing the copper plate

The preparation for using copper plate as an oil painting surface is not very well documented. The commonly mentioned preparation is rubbing garlic or garlic juice on the copper, having first roughened the surface. What does this do? Garlic is a powerful degreaser; it is sulphurous and possibly slightly bites the surface and then evaporates. Treatises say that it helps the oil paint to stick. My experience has shown that it also helps the paint to dry quicker, especially if the ground layer contains lead white.

Many paintings on copper have a ground layer that is beige — a mix of umber and white lead bound in oil. Two Spanish treatises, Pacheco's and the *Practica de la Pintura* (1724) of Palomino (1625–1726), describe a ground application for copper. They instruct that it should be an earth colour with white, in oil, applied after garlic; and they advise using the thumb or the ball of the hand to pound the paint in, so that it fills any imperfections in the surface caused by hammering or, if a plate has been used for printing, fills the depressions. This procedure, which has much in common with the way ink was applied, leaves a thin layer of paint all over the plate. Palomino says that smoothness can be enhanced by stroking the paint with a feather. I have tried this and it works beautifully at all stages of the painting.

Because paintings on copper are generally thinly painted, they are usually in a good state of preservation. Investigation of these paintings is so far limited. From examination of tiny paint samples from damaged areas it appears that there is often a green layer between the ground and the copper. It has not had an effect on the upper paint layers but indicates, perhaps, that the acidic oil used in a ground layer may react with the copper. I suggest that another type of ground layer may have been used that has not been detected by current investigative tools. Evidence of calcium carbonate, sulphate and white lead has been found and their presence could suggest the use of a gesso ground.

I do not remember what first prompted me to apply a gesso ground to copper but my own experiments with it have lasted a good few years. In theory one would think that gesso would not adhere to the metal but it does. It makes a lovely surface, smooth and silky, and perhaps too it creates a good barrier between the copper and the oil paint layers that follow it. This could have been an option that suited some seventeenth-century artists, but that is conjecture on my part. Unlike paint on canvas, the paint layer can only dry one way from the copper support and gesso ground — upwards. I don't know what the implications are of this.

Adam Elsheimer (1578–1610) did a number of night-time scenes that had a very dark ground. Rembrandt (1606–1669)

Above A portrait I painted on copper. The colour of the copper gives a luminous glow to the skin.
Below A painting after Elsheimer, by my pupil Victoria Hawkins

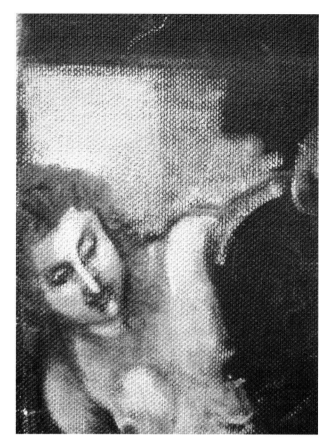 

Above left A figure modelled by putting in the lightest parts first, then pushing the paint around the shape into the dark ground

Above right A translucent grey veil might be painted over a gesso ground to modify the brightness of the white.

was one of several artists who experimented with coating the surface with gold or silver leaf, which harks back to fourteenth- and fifteenth-century panel painting practice, where the metals are reflective and decorative. The gold and silver on copper was sometimes glazed over with transparent layers of oil paint. Highlights or rays of gold were achieved by scratching through the oil paint layer to reveal gold.

Coloured grounds

The ground layer of the painting influences the tonality of the whole. In the fourteenth and fifteenth centuries the practice of using a white, light-reflecting gesso ground was almost universal. However, from the sixteenth century grounds on both panel and canvas were often coloured. And whereas the bright white of gesso on panel was, to put it simply, about drawing, colouring in and embellishments, oil painting on coloured grounds made for a different kind of richness of expression that was more about paint being enjoyed for its lusciousness and infinite variety of effects. Thick paint, thin paint, opaque or transparent – the colour of the ground layer affected all that was to follow.

Perhaps the use of light and dark grounds can be divided into north and south, the countries with the most sun using the darker grounds and the less sunny north continuing to favour lighter or mid-toned grounds.

Jacopo Tintoretto, *The Crucifixion of Christ*, 1565,
oil on canvas, 5360 × 12240 mm
Scuola Grande di San Rocco, Venice

The very dark grounds used in southern Europe in the sixteenth and seventeenth centuries could be anything from a warm earth colour to almost black. Really dark ground layers meant that the artist was working from dark to light: this was dramatic and faster for an artist working on a large scale, like Tintoretto or Caravaggio. The artist needed to design the picture on the dark ground using light paint or chalk: for a large painting the chalk would be attached to a long stick to facilitate working from a distance. The dark ground could be integral to the picture, giving the impression of mysterious depth with figures emerging from the darkness. The roundness of the figures was easily achieved by establishing the highest, lightest parts of a form and then pushing the paint around the form into the dark. As the paint recedes into the darkness it becomes thinner, creating a middle tone. This could be enriched with a transparent glaze.

For lighter, mid-toned grounds, a half-tone of pale yellow, greys and pinks was used. Sometimes an opaque or a translucent grey veil might be painted over the gesso. Artists did not stick rigidly to one colour throughout their career but adapted the ground to suit the colour layers predicted for the composition. It is not uncommon to find different ground layers on the one painting; for instance, it might suit the artist to have a different colour ground layer under skin.

Titian, *Bacchus and Ariadne*, 1522–23,
oil on canvas, 1760 × 1910 mm
National Gallery, London

Reconstructing Titian's Ariadne

Titian lived a long life (*c.* 1487–1576) and used a whole range of techniques, painting on panel, fresco and canvas. But when I was asked to demonstrate Titian's painting techniques for a television programme I knew at once that I wanted to paint the figure of Ariadne, from the wonderful *Bacchus and Ariadne* in the National Gallery in London. We know a lot about how this painting might have been made because there is a long and well-documented conservation history that is kept at the National Gallery.

I chose Ariadne because of her many colours. It is believed that in *Bacchus and Ariadne* Titian used practically every pigment available to the sixteenth-century artist — and Venice was the colour market of the world. I was particularly keen to use the lavish amounts of ultramarine and vermilion on Ariadne's drapery (especially as someone else was paying for the materials).

Preparation

First I stretched the canvas using the stringing method shown on page 100. We don't know if Titian stretched canvas like this, but it is a method that was commonly used in the sixteenth century. Then I sized the canvas with animal-skin glue.

When the glue had dried I used a brush and knife to apply gesso to fill the weave of the canvas. The canvas of *Bacchus and Ariadne* has gesso on both sides — a good idea as then the tension will be even. (We know this from a 1960s restoration when additional lining canvas layers were removed to reveal not just the gesso on the back but a little drawing too.) There is no evidence that Titian used a tinted primer in this painting. He seems to have worked directly on to the white gesso. It is worth bearing in mind, though, that after all these centuries the gesso may be greatly discoloured, and this would affect the colours to some extent.

Above The figure of Ariadne drawn up on blue paper

Below The image of Ariadne plotted on the canvas, with the beginning of the sea and sky

Planning the picture

There is much debate about how Titian set about designing his pictures: whether he made preparatory drawings or worked straight on to the canvas with his brush. Because oil paint dries slowly the design can be changed more readily than with quick-drying egg tempera, so it is not so important to have a carefully worked out drawing; Titian could be freer and more inventive than his predecessors. But Titian must have begun with lines and used sketches. Indeed infra-red photographs provide evidence that at least sometimes he or his assistants drew up. And how could we doubt this? It is important to remember that Titian ran a busy workshop producing many works, sometimes in more than one version. How do you instruct your assistants without drawing? It is true that there are few surviving drawings from Titian's workshop, but there could be various explanations for that. Drawings may simply have been lost in some misfortune. They could have been done on reusable surfaces or messed up by use in the studio.

For my Ariadne I worked out the figure — first naked, then draped — on paper and squared up the drawing, four times larger (see page 30). I transferred the drawing to the canvas, working first in charcoal, then fixing it in paint. I could have drawn from a model to get the pose or made a clay or wax model and drawn from that. This was common practice too and much recommended by Pacheco, who was a great admirer of

Titian and other artists of the high Renaissance in Italy. In fact, he said that an artist who doesn't do a great deal of rehearsal for a painting through drawing from life or models is lazy and usually not very good. He did say that among the exceptions was Tintoretto – whom Titian actually sacked from his studio!

Painting

We know from x-rays that while the figure of Bacchus seems to have been fixed early on, and painted in directly on the gesso, Titian changed the position of Ariadne. The x-rays show her as a swirling mass, which perhaps indicates that he had trouble with the twisting figure and changed it a lot. Tiny paint samples (cross-sections) suggest that she was painted over the ultramarine/white/azurite of the sea and sky.

I found it difficult to work out what colour to paint her flesh. The original, mellowed by time, looks delightfully creamy. The colour cross-section suggests a simple mix of white and red lake – very sugary. Cross-sections of paint, which are taken from the edges of cracks, are minute, fractions of a millimetre across, and it is possible that this one just doesn't include some of the pigments used. Cross-sections of other depictions of pale people in Titian paintings contain a mix of black, white, vermilion, red lake and some ochre. I experimented and found this looked much more convincing.

It was fun painting Ariadne's hair, all swirls and fine lines in a wonderful red-black. I used burnt sienna. I think Titian must have enjoyed this too, as he has made her hair a complex style and gorgeous colour.

Ariadne, painted in over the sea and sky

Ariadne's glorious hair, painted in burnt sienna

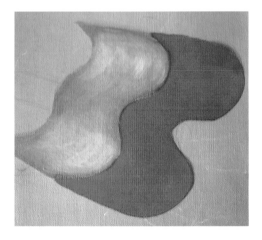 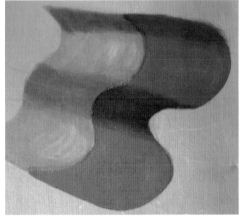 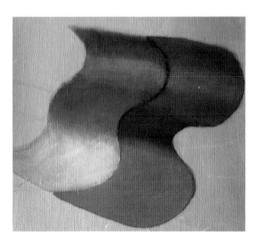

Showing the effect of transparent glazes over opaque layers, in folds in Ariadne's robes
From left to right Fold painted in ultramarine and vermilion, with white mixed into the paint on the convex peaks; with a transparent glaze of red lake in the hollow of the fold and on the top curved edge, to create a richer depth of colour; with a glaze of ultramarine over the whole of the top half, to give an even more luscious effect

The glorious blue and red drapery going across the body of Ariadne is painted in luscious, costly ultramarine blue and vermilion red. These pigments were obtained from a colour scientist, Dr Kremer of Germany, who specializes in manufacturing natural pigments in the traditional way. Once they were in the studio we treated them with appropriate reverence, mixing in the oil drop by drop – linseed for the vermilion and walnut oil (less yellowing) for the ultramarine – and then grinding to smoothness with a muller, just as Titian's assistants would have done. Both paints were quite difficult to apply, especially the ultramarine, which for all the grinding remained surprisingly gritty in texture: it was like working with sand. Getting the technique right took quite a lot of practice. But the result was an intensity and vibrancy of colour I have never achieved with modern pigments.

Glazing

The deeper folds of the blue drape are intensified by a glaze of ultramarine in stand oil and a bit of Venice turpentine. There may have been a red glaze on the scarf. None has so far been identified, but often opaque vermilion had a glaze of red lake (a translucent red dye extracted from cochineal beetles or lac insects, fixed on alum and mixed with oil). The glaze is used to great effect in folds by applying transparent over opaque. I glazed the shadows of the flesh tones by rubbing medium-rich ultramarine over the inside of the arm with my finger. The important thing with any glaze is that it must be applied over dry, opaque paint. Titian could have used any of a number of different methods of application. I am inclined to think that he may have used his fingers in some areas and a knife in others, especially with the really expensive colours. One wouldn't want them leaving costly residues in brushes. But perhaps Titian didn't worry about money.

Above left A detail showing the shadows created by rubbing an ultramarine glaze over the inside of the arm

Above right Showing the transparent blue glazes in the folds and the white scumbled highlights on top

The experience of re-creating Titian taught me even more respect for the way he painted. It also emphasized how important it is to know how to deal with the individual characteristics of each colour and medium.

Special effects

What could you do with oil paint that couldn't be done with quick-drying aqueous media like egg and gum? Oil paint gives tremendous flexibility. As it is slow to dry there is time to think and change your mind. Moreover, the drying rate can be varied by adding driers (siccatives from metal salts). As we have seen, glazes can give wonderful richness when applied over opaque colours. And artists would sometimes apply a flashy touch in the form of the quick flick of dryish paint known as a scumble. Titian did this for example in his painting of *Tarquin and Lucretia*, where he made highlights dance over the surface of Tarquin's pantaloons.

The plasticity of oil paint means that you can vary the thickness so long as you stick to the rule of fat over lean: thin paint dries quicker so the thicker paint comes last as it takes longer to dry – the reverse would be brittle. Oil paint can be thinned substantially with a diluent such as turpentine or spike or lavender oil to give a stain effect, although the oil binder must not be made so lean that the colour is barely held on the surface.

The finished painting of
Ariadne, after Titian

Right Titian, *Tarquin and Lucretia*, *c*. 1571, oil on canvas, 1889 × 1451 mm Note the white scumbled highlights on Tarquin's pantaloons. Fitzwilliam Museum, Cambridge

Opposite
Above left Rembrandt, *Self-portrait* (detail), *c*. 1665, oil on canvas, 1143 × 940 mm Kenwood House, London
Above right Frank Auerbach, *Head of EOW 1*, 1960, oil on wood, 433 × 355 mm, Tate, London

James McNeill Whistler (1834–1903) was an artist who explored the boundaries of oil paint. Influenced by Japanese prints and being a printmaker himself, he made up for a lack of technical knowledge by forcing the paint to bend to his will. He seemed to strive after a stain effect. Rather than have paint sit on top of canvas he wanted the paint to become one with the canvas. Years later this would be a preoccupation of artists like Mark Rothko and Morris Louis (see page 141). He was moving toward abstraction of his forms and expressionism. He created paint the consistency of salad dressing – he even referred to the mixture of pigment, varnish, turpentine and oil as his 'sauce'. This fluid mixture was easy to brush on and also to take off, as he strove to make an *a la prima* painting (*a la prima* means to paint in one go, rather than build up layers). Whistler was in the habit of wiping or scraping off areas of paint. This would leave a seductive shadow on which to try again.

Oil can also be manipulated to be thicker. It can, if the artist wishes, be built to a thick *impasto* (a paste). The paint is made thicker by the kind of oil and sometimes resin that is combined with the pigment. Certain pigments lend themselves to being made into impasto: lead white and earth colours, for example. Their presence in, say, flesh colour, or white on its own in a painting of white drapery, gives the paint extra body. Rembrandt's late self-portraits have rich impasto (especially about the nose), as does his *Belshazzar's Feast* in the National Gallery in London. A twentieth-century artist who went to extremes in the use of impasto is Frank Auerbach, whose impasto is so thick that it can stick out an inch from the surface; a new painting has to be delivered to his dealer lying horizontal, in a box.

Below My painting after Whistler, showing how thinned paint sinks into and stains the canvas

The changing palette

The changing palette

In addition to artists exploring the many and varied effects possible in oil paint, in the eighteenth, nineteenth and twentieth centuries there was a continuing search for new colours or variations on existing ones. Century by century the colour palette has been added to; and some pigments disappear or become less popular because of their difficulty of use, availability or toxicity.

Changes in how artists' materials were manufactured made them not only more convenient to use but also, by the nineteenth century, available to amateur artists as well. The increased availability of education, including academies in the eighteenth century and art and design schools in the nineteenth, plus the rise of a new middle class who had leisure time to indulge in art, meant that there was a market for more artists' materials. Technologies combined with developments in colour chemistry and commercial competition – as manufacturers discovered there was money to be made – introduced a whole new range of artists' products, making different ways of working possible.

The explosion of industrialization affected the production of everything. The elements zinc, cadmium, chrome and cobalt could be manipulated to produce a range of yellows, reds, greens and blues that could be standardized in a way that natural pigments could not. Competition was international and during the nineteenth century colours were patented in ever-increasing numbers. Many of the new colours were by-products of other industries such as ceramics and cloth-dyeing. Coal tar was a by-product of the gas and coal industry and produced a whole range of dyes used for cloth and (terrifyingly) food colouring. The big challenge was to find a substitute for blue from lapis lazuli. It was in France that this – like so many of the new colours – was successfully synthesized, and a French chemist beat off all competitition from other countries to patent it as French ultramarine. This was created from a combination of soda, silica, sulphur and alumina. It was much cheaper than lapis lazuli and is still the most popular blue.

Joshua Reynolds (1723–1792) – an artist so fixated on understanding the art of the past that he is rumoured to have deconstructed a Titian in the hope of understanding how it was composed – had a fondness for bitumen, a transparent brown pigment derived from tar that was useful for shadowing. He used it far too liberally and today evidence can be seen in his paintings of the scaly, crusty effect that results from its overuse. His contemporary Thomas Gainsborough (1727–1788) also used bitumen, but in a much more conservative way so his paintings did not end up looking like alligator skin.

The palette of J.M.W. Turner (1775–1851) straddled the old and the new. Much of his work and some of his palettes and equipment are preserved at Tate Britain. On display there are colours still in bladders (the forerunner of the tube, made from the tough membrane of pig's bladder), others in the new-fangled tubes, and little glass phials of dry pigment, some of them the newer pigments which he is said to have embraced as they became available. His painting *The Hero of a Hundred Fights* has a large swirling sun made with chrome yellow.

J. M. W. Turner,
The Hero of a Hundred Fights,
c. 1800–1810, oil on canvas,
908 × 1213 mm
Tate, London

In England in 1856 a very clever young chemist, William Perkin, created mauve in his bedroom laboratory and at eighteen became the richest chemist in England (his story is the subject of a book called *Mauve*). It was the strongest mauve colour ever produced without mixing two colours together, and it was used both for dyeing fabric and for artists' paint. It was much beloved of the English Pre-Raphaelites.

With the invention of the tube in the 1840s, for the first time artists could take their paints outside. They could take a kit of folding easels, seats, boxes containing tubes of paint, little bottles of oils and diluents, brushes and small canvases. Without these things the Impressionists would not have been able to make impressions of lights and colour in the open air.

In England companies like Winsor and Newton, Rowney, Brodie and Middleton and Roberson had retail outlets. This convenience meant that artists no longer had to make their own paints, and they became removed from knowing about the materials that they were using.

William Holman Hunt,
Claudio and Isabella, 1850,
oil on mahogany,
758 × 426 mm
Tate, London

The death of painting again

New colours, tools and trains

The group of artists who became known as the Impressionists acquired the name as an insult from critics who found their anti-academic, 'unfinished' work unacceptable for the prevailing tatste of the day. The academies, who had a rigid system of education and studio-based art featuring dull colours and limited subject matter, were becoming stale and turning in on themselves. This situation was stifling for the young, who wanted to find their own mode of expression using the new materials of the industrial age. Keen to explore their individuality apart from the academies, they set up their own studios

Claude Monet, *The Beach at Trouville*, 1870,
oil on canvas, 380 × 460 mm
National Gallery, London

and salons to challenge the old order. Courbet, Cézanne, Monet, Van Gogh, Degas and *women*, Berthe Morisot and Mary Cassatt, were some of the main protagonists. They so wanted a breath of fresh air that they literally took painting outside, where they revelled in the light and vibrant colours, recording and reacting to nature. For city dwellers the countryside was now easily accessible by train.

Impressionism was mainly a French movement. At the same time in England, the Pre-Raphaelites were in the ascendant. They were aware of and influenced by France, but the less favourable climate kept them more often indoors, creating fantasies, histories and paintings featuring moral tales with Victorian values. They too benefited from and adopted the new colours and materials.

Brushes

The kind of marks that the Impressionists and their followers were able to make was dependent on the shape of the brush and the type of hair used. In the nineteenth century, for the first time artists had a wide choice of brush shape. Flat, square-ended, filbert (a sort of pointed spade shape) and fan shapes were made. Usually the hairs were squeezed into a metal ferule (the part of a brush that holds the hair at one end, the other fitting on to the handle). Made, like the tube, of easily manipulated metal, the brush ferule could be shaped to fit a round or flattened form. These new brush shapes, and the use of stiff hog-hair brushes rather than soft sable, facilitated the mottling and dabbing of patches of colour that characterize Impressionist brushstrokes. Soft-hair brushes continued to be used both for oil paint and in particular for the delicate art of watercolour painting, which became popular in the nineteenth century. (For more on soft-hair brushes, see pages 130–32.)

Palettes

Palettes of many shapes and sizes have been devised to suit different situations. It surprises me that really only the miniaturists, illuminators and watercolour painters use a palette of a colour and texture related to the surface on which they work, that is, cream or white. Oil painters in particular tend to set out their colours on a brown wooden palette that is usually quite different from the painting surface. Why? It would make sense always to work on a surface the same colour as the ground layer of the picture.

At one side of the palette are tubes of paint, and at the other old-fashioned bladders. In between is a selection of brushes.
From left to right Square-ended brush, flat, a fan, two filberts and a round stippling brush. The fan, used for blending, is sable; all the other brushes are hog-hair.

A language of colour

Not all the new colours were reliable, and quality control was not consistent. The Impressionists, Post-Impressionists and Pointillistes (or Divisionists) all encountered problems with durability. Like all the Impressionists and Post-Impressionists, Georges Seurat (1859–1891) was very interested in colour theories. From the beginning of his career Seurat sought an optical system that could be used to make his pictures – a modern language of colour. He and his friends were influenced by the colour theories of Charles Chevreul, Charles Henri and the American Ogden Rood. These were a development from the theories of Isaac Newton and Goethe, a mélange of quasi-scientific notions about how placing complementary colours next to each other (rather than mixing them with each other), the after-image experienced and the emotional impact all contributed to the viewer's perception of colours. After his early death at the age of thirty-two Seurat's followers, notably Paul Signac (1863–1935), continued to explore what became known as Pointillism. In the 1960s, Bridget Riley – who, in her youth, copied one of Seurat's paintings – developed Op Art, a style which dazzled and manipulated the eye/brain in a way that seems directly linked to Pointillism.

Georges Seurat, *Sunday Afternoon on the Island of La Grande Jatte*, 1884–86,
oil on canvas, 2075 × 3080 mm
Art Institute of Chicago

Re-creating a Seurat

Seurat did his painting *La Grande Jatte* twice. He painted it first as an Impressionist and then he went over it as a Pointillist. There were two distinct 'campaigns' of painting. In the first he used much broader brushstrokes, in the second smaller dots and dashes of carefully chosen tones that wove together like tweed to give a shimmering effect of light.

For several years he built up to this iconic painting, making many drawings and oil sketches of all its elements. They were mostly made on the river bank opposite the spot where he had painted his previous equally large composition *The Bathers*. A large cast of characters was involved and he rehearsed their shapes, sizes, costumes and positions like a theatre or film director creating a scene. Many years later this did not escape Stephen Sondheim, who took the painting as inspiration for his musical *Sunday in the Park with George*. Seurat made the final painting in his studio, where it took up the whole of the end wall. He painted under artificial light. The constancy of the light, uninterrupted by the confusion of natural light changes, would have been useful in the application of his colour language.

In the second phase of the painting he applied carefully calculated colour combinations all over the surface, using dots and dashes in different sizes and going in different directions. Some dashes described forms. The brightest yellow that he used was zinc yellow; combined with white it was the nearest he could get to sunlight. He also mixed it with greens and reds, so that all his colours were opaque. Seurat did not live to witness the major colour changes that affected *La Grande Jatte* within a couple of years of its completion. Any colour with zinc yellow in it turned to a weird dark colour. The grass, which contains pinks, oranges and greens, now has what look like nasty holes in it where zinc yellow strokes or dots had been. The painting must have been singing with sunlight before this happened.

Conté crayon drawing of Seurat's fishing lady, after one of the preparatory drawings for *La Grande Jatte*

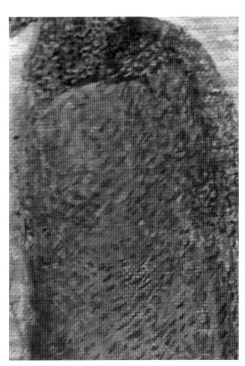

Far left A detail of *La Grande Jatte*, after Seurat, emulating the larger, looser, Impressionist brushstrokes of the first painting campaign
Left A re-creation of the smaller dots and dashes of the second campaign, applying the colour theories of Pointillism

Lady fishing, from my reconstruction, after Seurat
Below left First campaign
Below right Second campaign

Detail of the head
Below First campaign
Bottom Second campaign

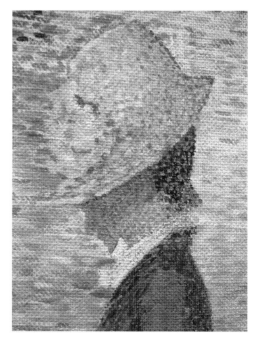

To show the difference between the two campaigns of painting and to see what the colours might have looked like before the changes occurred, I re-created a part of *La Grande Jatte* — the lady fishing on the river bank — in its two stages. In this reconstruction I tried to use the same palette as Seurat (based on analysis of the painting by the Art Intitute of Chicago): chrome orange, zinc yellow, vermilion, cobalt blue, purple, viridian green, emerald. Seurat mixed white with almost everything, believing it increased the vibrancy of the colours. By the time he painted *La Grande Jatte* he had eliminated black and earth colours from his palette, believing that they killed other colours and didn't vibrate.

The skirt is mainly orange strokes but within it there are juxtapositions of blue dots and dashes. The combination of light blue and orange gives a much stronger impression of orange light on the surface, completed by the brain. You know they are two distinct colours but they work together as one. I don't know why he used pink within the red, blue, orange, yellow combination: it is puzzling as it doesn't seem to have a function in the way that some other combinations add to the flickerability of the surface.

My experience of trying to emulate Seurat's painting was painful, as exposure to the constant dazzle of the shimmer from the colours induces headache . . . like staring at the heat haze of a summer's day. I could not imagine how Seurat managed to paint in this way for long hours. Did he have help? The purity of his colour mixes was very important and I wondered whether he kept a brush for each colour. The size of the painting was so large: did he use a ladder and did he lie on the floor for the lower bits?

Seurat imposed a unique discipline of his own on the surface of the painting. In *La Grande Jatte* he is trying to do many things, colours bouncing on and off surfaces, different strokes and even haloes of fluorescence around figures. Perhaps they don't all succeed but what the viewer witnesses is an artist taking risks, exploring a process, inventing a language.

Is this the only painting to have been re-created in topiary (in Columbus, Ohio)?

Far left and left Details of the dress and the grass from my reconstruction of the second campaign, showing the shimmering/ vibrating effect of the mix of colours and strokes, like a scattering of hundreds and thousands

Watercolours

Watercolours

Watercolour paint made from gum, sugar, glycerine and, occasionally, ear wax and honey has been used for centuries. It was the medium for illuminated manuscripts and miniatures. As far back as the sixteenth century watercolour painting was recommended as part of a gentleman's education. However, watercolour paints and painting came into their own in the eighteenth and especially the nineteenth centuries. They were quick-drying and portable and – rather important for some – washable. A genteel lady practising the art of watercolour painting need not worry about spoiling her clothes as she would have to when using oil paints. Queen Victoria was a keen watercolourist.

Little blocks of ready-to-use colour were manufactured to cater not just for the professional artist but also for the increasing number of amateur painters. Everything to do with watercolour painting was on a small scale: blocks of special papers that would take a water-based paint, little sets of colours and palettes, fine sable brushes. The only other constant requirement was water, to moisten the cakes of colour and clean brushes. Fastidiousness in keeping paints, water and brushes clean is essential to this medium. There is also little opportunity for alterations, as they are likely to show. A skilled painter, though, can sometimes remove sections by washing out, provided the paper is tough enough.

Paper

Artists of the eighteenth and nineteenth centuries had a wider choice of handmade papers than ever before. There were papers used for writing and drawing on and generally tougher papers for painting on with water-based media. These were quite different from the parchment that was used for documents and books.

Paper suitable as a support for painting was made mostly of rags. Basically old cotton, linen or hemp fabrics were sorted into coloured and not coloured, and then washed and beaten to a pulp. These fabrics are all made from vegetable fibres. Paper can be and is also made directly from plant fibres. It is the cellulose fibres that are the important ingredient; these are changed by being broken down and re-formed to become paper. The rags are washed and beaten to a pulp and then they are spread out on metal mesh sheet moulds and the moisture is squashed out. When the fibres are loosely melded together they are tipped on to felt sheets and squashed so that excess water is removed. Some papers are then dried and have no further treatment: they are known as Rough; others are squeezed further and called Not, meaning Not Hot-pressed, which is the final category, when the still-damp paper is squashed between hot metal sheets to produce smooth Hot-pressed paper.

Depending on where the paper has been made, it will have the maker's mark pressed into it; this is visible when the sheet is held up to the light. The mark is formed in the wires of the mesh. Also visible in early papers are rows of chain marks from the mesh. Papers with this mark are known as 'laid'. Papers that do not have the chain pattern are known as 'wove', because their mesh mould is made from woven wires.

Paper of different textures.

From left to right Rough, Not and Hot-pressed

After the paper has been dried for about a month a gelatine size is applied to the surface. This is a more refined animal-glue size than that used to seal canvas. Without a size coat the ink or watercolour paint would bleed. Sugar paper is unsized and therefore not suitable for working on in wet media.

A peculiarly English medium

The English landscape was much celebrated in the nineteenth century, especially during the Napoleonic wars, when worries about invasion and restrictions on foreign travel inclined artists to romantically celebrate bucolic England. Perhaps too the increasing industrialization of towns and cities made people appreciate the landscape.

Artists like J.M.W. Turner, John Sell Cotman (1782–1842) and William Blake (1757–1827) used watercolour to great effect. Turner in particular exploited the medium to the fullest extent. He used both transparent watercolour paints and gouache (which is watercolour that is opaque, either because the pigment itself is opaque or because white has been added to the pigment, to make it opaque). Turner also used a variety of papers to suit different situations, and sometimes he tinted the surface to minimize the whiteness so that he could scratch into it to make highlights. In pushing the medium of watercolour out of its more typical application of transparent paint over white paper that reflects light, he was an innovator ahead of his time. He lived in a period when there was little division

J.M.W. Turner, *Rainbow over Loch Awe*, c. 1831,
pencil and watercolour on paper, 225 × 286 mm
Private collection

between science and art and travelled abroad where he met up with his friends, the natural philosophers (as scientists were then called) Humphry Davy, Michael Faraday and Mary Somerville. They were all able amateur artists and Mary Somerville was an accomplished watercolourist. Turner and his friends were keen to record and understand extreme weather conditions, rainbows, lightning, storms. Turner is said to have strapped himself to the mast of a boat in order to record a storm at sea.

Until the nineteenth century oil paint was accepted as the most serious medium for artists and those who favoured watercolour were considered lesser artists. It was all right to use watercolour for on-the-spot sketches to be worked up later in the studio, but it took the establishment of organizations like the Society of Painters in Water Colour (1801), the New Society of Painters in Watercolour (1831) and eventually, in the 1860s, the Royal Society of Painters in Watercolour for the medium to be taken seriously. The setting up of separate exhibitions was a challenge to the Royal Academy, where watercolours, although admitted, were generally hung where they would not be appreciated and attract buyers.

Brushes

For making fine watercolours, brushes need to be of the best quality. We can all remember the horror of using ghastly, dirty brushes at school. The hairs often fell out and they didn't retain a point. Really good brushes are expensive and should be cared for like the finest cashmere; in fact, a manufacturer that I spoke with said you shouldn't do anything to your brush that you would not do to your own hair. Think mink and sable: that is the kind of hair that is most suitable. Fur coats can withstand cold and wet, but they need to be respected and cared for. The same is true of the best sable brushes. There is nothing like sable. No synthetic or mixed natural and synthetic brush is as satisfactory to use with watercolour. The more you pay the better the brush. Renowned throughout the world and possibly the best for watercolour are Winsor and Newton's Series 7 brushes. Great skill goes into their making and the raw ingredients are costly and come from parts of the world where the climate is tough and produces animals with hardy fur, like the Kolinsky sable that is found in Siberia.

I had the privilege of visiting the factory where Series 7 are made and saw the process from beginning to end. The factory has been based at Lowestoft for over fifty years. Lowestoft was chosen because there was a tradition among a mainly female workforce of using the clove hitch knot for making fishing nets. The dexterity needed for this knot transferred easily to securing the hairs on brushes.

Most brushmakers learn how to carry out all stages of the brushmaking process. Training starts with practising knot tying.

The making of a brush

1. Hair from the side of the tail of a sable is cut from the stump, ready for combing and sorting. The tip of the tail is not used for fine brushes because it may be damaged and blunt from catching on abrasive surfaces. The tips do, however, probably find their way into poorer-quality brushes.
2. Guard hairs are the longer hairs with a point; they offer protection from wet, as the water rolls off. The wool, the lower part nearest the skin, provides warmth. (A brilliant design.) The two kinds of hair are separated with a comb.
3. The hairs are sorted into lengths of hair for different kinds of brushes. Shorter hairs are used for making shorter brushes, which are used as spotters, for making tiny dots, or by miniaturists. They form a good point but hold less paint in their belly.
4. The hairs are put into a brass gun cartridge case so that they may be tapped down to form bundles.
5. The bundles are wrapped in acid-free cartridge paper and several bundles are tied together ready for sterilizing, drying and ironing.

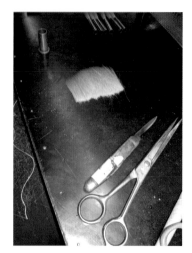

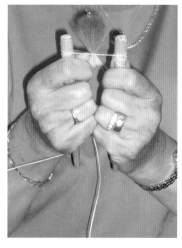

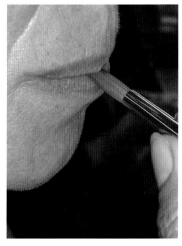

6. Each bundle is divided and the hairs are tied and inserted into a metal ferule.

7. The base ends are trimmed and the points are tested and set with paste.

8. The handle of the brush is attached and the points are tested in clear water. Those that pass are now ready for packaging. An experienced assembler can produce over a hundred size 8 sable brushes in a day.

Now will you look after your brushes?

A child could do that

Toward the end of his life Henri Matisse (1869–1954) made many wonderful works using gouache. Matisse had used all kinds of material for his work. He strove always for a way of capturing colour and in his late cut-outs he achieved a way of colour being of itself. Scissors, paper and paste replaced paint, brushes and canvas.

After the end of the Second World War, Picasso (1881–1973) and Françoise Gilot visited Matisse in Vence. They were amazed to see him sitting up in bed wielding a large pair of scissors, slicing through painted paper at great speed, as though drawing. Gilot said that the bravura performance stunned Picasso into silence.

Matisse had been using scissors to 'draw' since the 1930s when he used cut-outs to plan works by arranging shapes prior to painting. By the 1940s and 1950s the cut-outs were used in their own right. Matisse had his assistants paint out large sheets of paper in strong colours. He would not have been able to buy what he wanted ready-made. He then created shapes with his scissors and his assistants arranged pieces under his direction. *The Snail*, completed the year before he died in 1954, still has pin marks where shapes were pinned prior to sticking.

The paper needed to be stiff enough to hold paint but not so strong that his hands could not support the paper and the scissors. He used sheets of Canson paper, which was Not – that is, paper that has not been made smooth. Typically, watercolour painters prefer paper that has a texture. This can be slight or quite pronounced.

For his cut-out pictures Matisse found that the Linel brand of gouache paint was the best because its colours could be matched to printing inks. This was particularly important and successful when his gouaches were to be translated into print for the limited edition folio book *Jazz* in 1947. Another reason for using Linel was that it claimed to be light-fast. (At this time Matisse was rather proud that his oculist warned him his eyes were being over-stimulated by the intensity of his colours.) Examination of *The Snail* by the Tate in 1978 showed that the colours were still not faded.

Some might perceive the late cut-out pictures by Matisse as infantile: they have prompted the comment 'a child could do that', so often applied to things that look simple. The cut-outs were the culmination of a lifetime's exploration, a journey where each stopping point was the development of a new way of working. It was as though he was cutting out the middle man and creating in a far more direct way, not impeded by the physical paraphernalia of painting. No need for paint-mixing, brushes and palette. No need for boundaries or movements. No need to justify. His facility with scissors enabled him to release the essence of his creativity in a blaze of colour, shape and movement. With the cut-outs he seemed to transcend his troubles and his physical infirmities, and make what he described as 'the graphic, linear equivalent of the sensation of flight'.

Matisse, *Icarus* from *Jazz*, published
1947, pochoir print on paper, page size
420 × 655 mm, image size 420 × 327 mm
Scottish National Gallery
of Modern Art, Edinburgh

Trying to make a small version of *The Snail* was revelatory. What looks like a really simple composition had unexpected elements.

I followed the description of its making as understood by the Tate conservation team who assessed it and wrote about it in a publication called *Completing the Picture*.

According to them, Kraft paper (a strong brown paper) was glued to the face of a ready-stretched canvas. This would have provided a base and a protection for the Canson and Mongolfier white paper that was to form the background for the shapes. The Kraft paper stopped any canvas weave from showing through and, according to the Tate, it would minimize the distortion caused by fluctuations of movement. I was making a very small version (the original is 2850 × 2870 mm). I tried applying the two layers of paper separately, first the Kraft paper to canvas and then the white paper on to the Kraft. Attaching the two layers in this way caused bumps in the surface as the layers dried at different rates. Applying paste to the canvas and to the two papers and then pressing them on to the surface simultaneously worked perfectly.

Re-creating Matisse's *Snail*

I stretched eight pieces of wet Canson paper on to a board with brown paper tape and when they were flat and dry I painted each piece with one of the colours.

I coated the white surface with white gouache and then traced the shapes from a book and enlarged them to fit the base. I cut or tore each shape according to how I understood the order of application by observing the painting at Tate Modern. The sequence can be seen from the illustration. There was nothing random about the positioning: each shape and colour had its value. I think *The Snail* is analogous to music or dance, it vibrates and moves. A child could not do that.

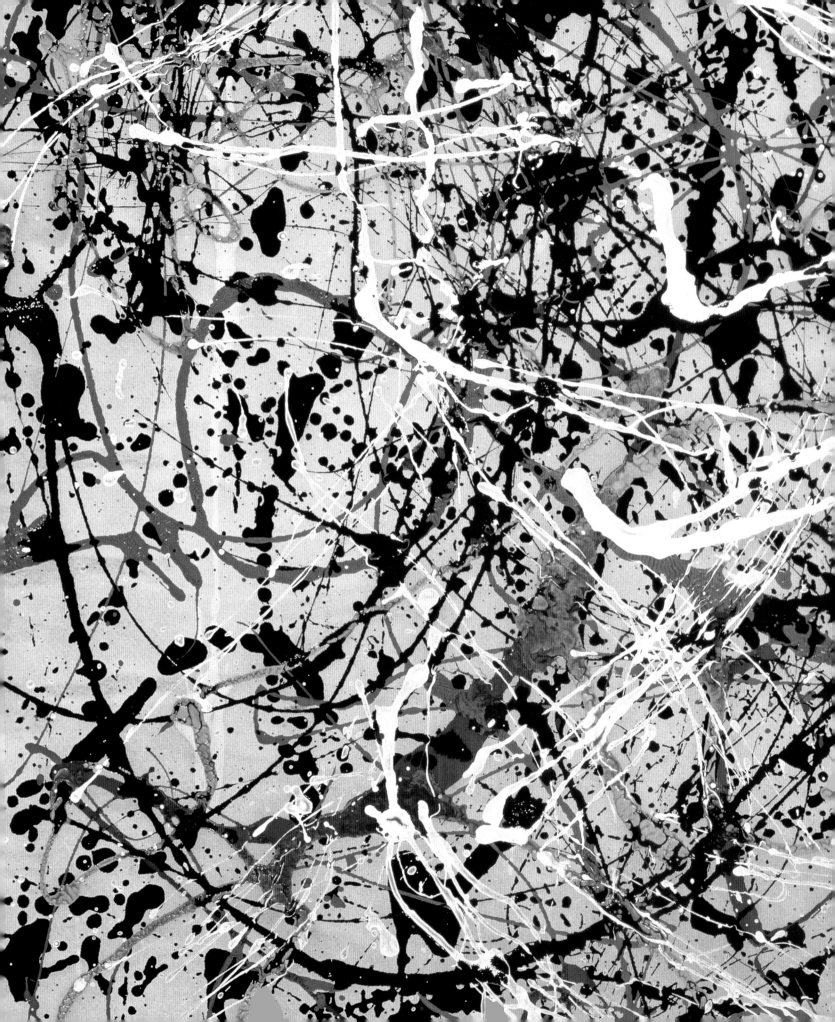

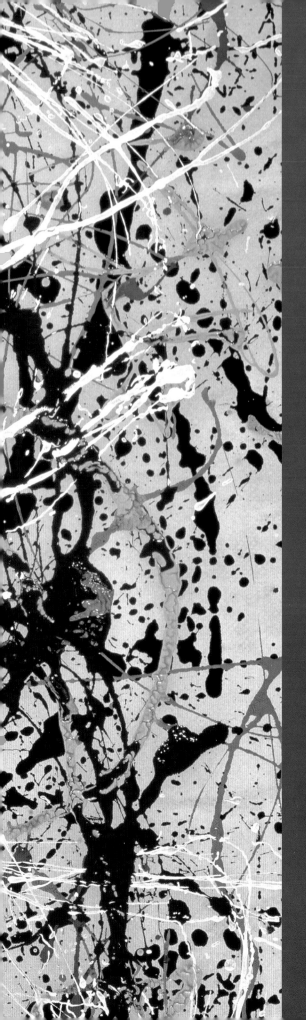

Acrylics

Acrylics

In the twentieth century artists were freed from any constraints in terms of what they chose to make their work from or about. Today anything is possible, from using electronic media to preserving sharks in formaldehyde. Artists who worked in new, non-traditional ways required new materials, as the old ones did not work for them. Of course there were and continue to be artists who want to use paint as a vehicle for their ideas; and they turned to new types of paint.

Many artists in the first half of the twentieth century wanted to work at speed on a large scale; for them, paint that dried quickly was desirable. The development of acrylics was a boon for those who wanted to paint large areas of flat colour that either formed a film or stained into the surface. Acrylics could be applied thick or thin, opaque or transparent. They could also be manipulated with different additives that varied the consistency to suit; they could be like a paste or a liquid and contained in jars, tins, bottles or tubes. The use of acrylics was a major change, perhaps more dramatic than any previous developments in artists' paints, and it happened over a relatively short time.

What are acrylics?

Acrylic resins are synthetic binding media. They are used instead of traditional binders: egg, oil and natural resins. They did not replace the traditional media but in the twentieth century they increased the choice of working methods available to artists. Synthetic resins copy the action of natural media in a form that is more convenient to use, and this suited the way some artists wanted to work. The scientists and – in some cases – non-scientists who developed acrylic paints could get them to do what artists needed. Sometimes changes were made as the result of discussions with artists: for example, paint manufacturer Leonard Bocour altered the consistency of the paint and the size of container as a response to what artists told him.

Europe had always been at the forefront of the commercial development of more traditional artists' materials, but in the twentieth century America led the way in acrylics. Perhaps their development was accelerated by the needs of mass production; in particular the emergent car industry needed fast-drying, hard-finish coatings. Some artists were keen to use all the new paints, whether they were for artists, cars, or houses, sometimes combining them all and sometimes to detrimental effect, as not all the paints were compatible.

In the 1940s and 1950s there were two types of acrylic paint. One was approximately 40 per cent resin solids dissolved in a solvent such as turpentine or toluene and wax. The pigment was mixed with this and produced quite a stiff paint. The manufacturer, Leonard Bocour, then added to his paint range a more liquid paint by excluding wax and increasing the resin content to 50 per cent. This suited artists who wanted to throw the stuff around a bit and work on a large scale.

The other kind of acrylic paint was an emulsion. This did not require a smelly, toxic solvent and was therefore healthier to use – not that anybody worried much about the

David Hockney, *A Bigger Splash*, 1967,
acrylic on canvas, 2425 × 2439 mm
Tate, London

toxicity of the paint in the early days. The resin, in fine particle form, coalesces round the pigment particles to make a liquid paint that can also be thinned with water. Unlike watercolour paints, which remain re-soluble after drying, water-based acrylics dry to an insoluble film, which means that layers can be painted on top of each other in a very short time. Perhaps a simple way of explaining the difference between the two main types of acrylic paints is to compare them to the kind of household paints we use that are categorized as emulsion, which is water-based, and gloss, which is solvent-based. But in truth there is a multitude of combinations based on synthetic resins.

David Hockney (b. 1937) used acrylics for years. They suited the kind of work he did for a while. In his autobiography, *Hockney on Hockney,* he described how he used them. He liked them for pictures with large areas of sky, lawns and water. He found that adding washing-up liquid to the paint made it absorb into the cotton canvas

Morris Louis, *Aleph Series 1*, 1960,
acrylic resin on canvas, 2670 × 3604 mm
Private collection

rather than sitting on top. This was especially good when he was painting his swimming pool pictures because the liquid paint was like the water he was painting. Leonard Bocour told him of this trick, which was also used by the older generation of painters in acrylics, including Morris Louis (1912–1962), Kenneth Noland (b. 1924) and Helen Frankenthaler (b. 1928).

Reconstructing a Veil, after Morris Louis

I tried following the sequence of one of Morris Louis' *Veil* paintings as described by conservators at Tate Britain.

First I tacked the cotton canvas out on a stretcher with loose gathers/pleats.

Then I poured red paint on the canvas from the top and tilted it each way so that the paint would run into the folds. At first the paint didn't want to adhere and separated into globules. I brushed some solvent on to the canvas and tried again; this time the paint was absorbed.

I unpinned the canvas to achieve a different effect as I poured orange and yellow followed by green on to it, creating a 'bleed'. By wiping or brushing solvent into the paint I leached out some of the colour. All the painting/staining was done wet in wet.

I don't know whether this was exactly how Louis worked but it was the method I followed, based on the information I had. I enjoyed the pure abstract, controlled accident of the process.

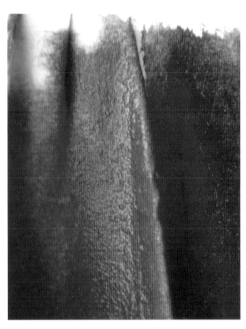

The pleated cotton

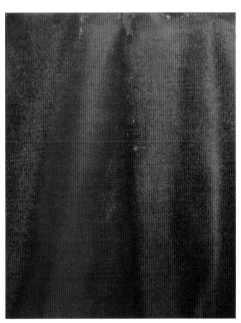

Liquid red poured and manipulated by tilting to distribute the paint in the folds

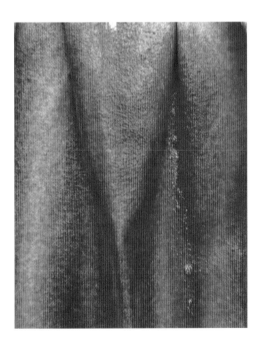

Yellow and orange added wet in wet to bleed into the red

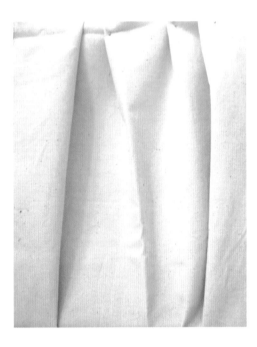

Green added, then lighter areas created by dribbling solvent to spread the wet paint and leach out some of the colour

Who made the paints?

Compared to the slow evolution of egg tempera and oil as media the development of acrylics was fast. It was also recent enough for us to know something of the people who developed them. Liquitex and Magna were the trade names of the first manufacturers of acrylics in America.

Although acrylic resin was first developed in Germany by Otto Rohm in 1901 it was not until the 1930s and 1940s that it was developed for artists. Henry Levison's Permanent Pigments, which made a product called Liquitex, was founded in 1935, and Leonard Bocour began trading Magna colours in 1947. Jackson Pollock (1912–1956), Kenneth Noland, Morris Louis and Helen Frankenthaler were all early users of acrylic paints and were able to develop their stain technique using Bocour's Magna paint.

Levison was a chemist; Bocour was a former art student who happened to get involved with the great wave of postwar American artists. Paint-making became a lucrative business, and there are now many different makers offering a variety of synthetic-resin paint products.

Leonard Bocour

Bocour would never have thought of becoming an artists' colourman had he not met an artist called Emil Ganzo (1895–1941). The teenage Bocour had gone to various art classes in New York with a friend whose cousin was married to Ganzo. This was the first time that Bocour had met an artist, and hanging around Ganzo's studio he would watch as he ground his own pigments in oil. Good artists' oil paints were mainly imported from Europe, so they were expensive, and Ganzo, who was of German descent, was not satisfied with American-manufactured oil paints, which was why he ground his own. Bocour was soon helping him to do this. Then when Bocour was sacked from a job in advertising, with little work available during the 1930s Depression, Ganzo suggested that he could make paint for artists commercially. Bocour started to sell his own hand-ground paints by going round artists' studios. He graduated to having a small shop and competed with imports from Winsor and Newton, offering his paints at prices a third lower than theirs. In 1941 a man came into Bocour's shop with a pot of synthetic resin that he said was called acrylic, saying 'It's swell stuff.' This meeting heralded the beginning of experiments to turn acrylic into a workable medium for paint.

Bocour met a number of artists through the Federal Art Projects. The Projects, as they were known, were set up as part of President Franklin D. Roosevelt's New Deal scheme to combat the economic downturn during the Depression; through them artists were paid a small amount to produce artworks for public places. The kind of work that was chosen was, according to Bocour, almost all in a Socialist Realist style, depicting happy workers (which is ironic considering that the Depression meant people didn't have any work) and weeping mothers. But, Bocour said, the Projects were a wonderful training ground for artists, where they learned to use paints, and were given the materials and some money to sustain themselves. Bocour got to provide the paints for some of these projects and at the same time met the artists, who, once no longer involved in the Projects, abandoned the accepted style and experimented with non-representational work – Abstraction, Expressionism and Action Painting. Among them were Willem de Kooning (1904–1997), Mark Rothko (1903–1970), Morris Louis and Jackson Pollock, who went on to develop their own distinctive interests that made them world renowned.

Bocour missed being called up into the army during the Second World War because he failed a medical, as a back injury sustained after being struck by lightning left him with a lack of reflex in his foot. He said in an interview that he really wanted to fight Fascism; but the army's loss was art's gain, as he was able to develop his paint business. Bocour colours in various forms are still available worldwide. Bocour's generosity to artists early on in their careers in giving them paints to try and also listening to their needs as he developed his products resulted in his acquiring a collection of over four hundred mid-twentieth-century masterpieces, many of them gifts from the artists.

Tools and materials

It was a free-for-all as far as tools for acrylics were concerned: anything might be used to apply the new paints. They could be applied with traditional soft sables, though this was a bit of a waste. Hog would do too. But after the Second World War synthetic brushes were developed to imitate natural pig hairs. Initially they did not handle as well but gradually they have become far more suitable for acrylics than natural hair brushes. Technologies have been developed to make brushes that re-form their shape after washing.

Artists using acrylics tended to work on the cheaper cotton duck canvas. It was creamy white as distinct from the grey/beige of the much more expensive linen or hemp canvas. The colour of the cotton duck could be integral to the painting. Painters sometimes used it, rather ill-advisedly, without any primings. Acrylics were also painted on all sorts of other supports, including hardboard, MDF and metal.

There are advantages and disadvantages to working on cotton duck. Tensions and ripples were sometimes created because the paint was stiffer and stronger than the fabric. The fabric was also affected by fluctuations in humidity. White areas get dirty and are difficult to clean. A cotton curtain would get dirty just hanging and a painting with bare areas of cotton left unpainted will get dirty too, absorbing dirt particles in interstices between the threads, as acrylic paintings are often not protected by varnish. Fingermarks are not easy to eradicate. The new material and ways of working with it present a lot of new problems for conservators that are now being researched.

Acrylics handle very differently from either oil paint or egg tempera. Artists who thought they could use them in the same way as traditional materials were mistaken. They feel different and they do not mix with each other in the same way as oil paint. Effects like glazing and impasto are achievable but require specific separate media. There is a range of extra products – for example, thinners, thickeners and retarders – to buy and learn how to use, You could not have the convenience of acrylics without adapting your working method. It really was a new paint for a new way of working and needed to be understood.

I helped make New York the art capital of the world.
Leonard Bocour,
interview with Paul Cummings, 1978

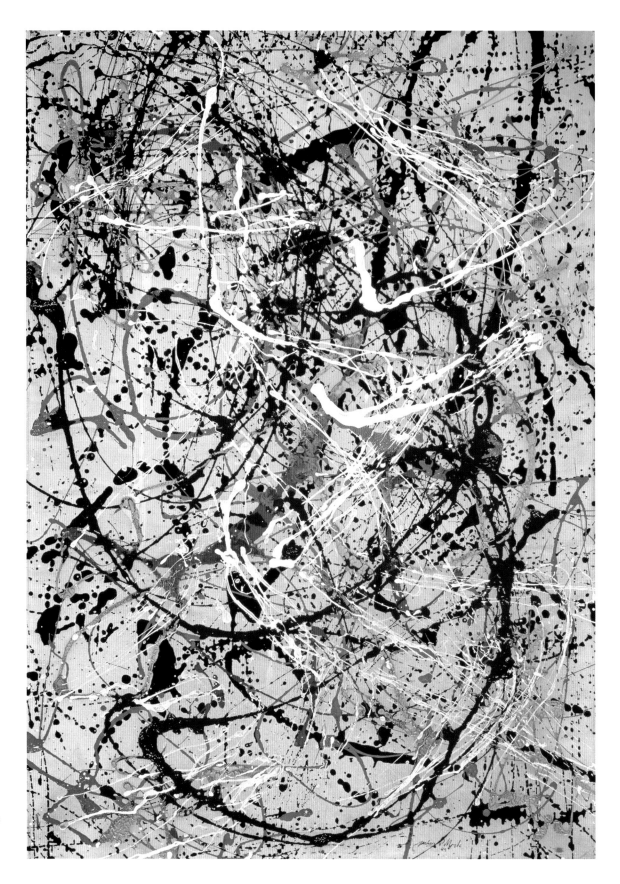

Jackson Pollock, *Number 20*,
1949, enamel on paper laid on
masonite, 700 × 490 mm.
Private collection

How Jackson Pollock painted

During the Second World War gloss enamel paints were more readily available and cheaper than artists' oil paints. Pollock described his use of modern household and industrial paints, as well as artists' oil paints, as 'a natural growth out of a need'.

Pollock wanted his abstract expressionist canvases to dance, with him as the highly involved dancer/choreographer. His canvases were mainly large, often worked on the floor with him dancing over the surface, pouring and dripping a mixture of thinned liquid house paint and oil paint. In 1947 he explained to the magazine *Possibilities*: 'On the floor I am more at ease. I feel nearer, more part of the painting, since this way I can walk around it, work from the four sides, and literally be *in* the painting.' The artist Lee Krasner, who was married to Pollock, described his palette as 'typically a can or two of … enamel, thinned to the point he wanted it, standing on the floor besides the rolled-out canvas'. She said that Pollock used Duco or Davoe and Reynolds brands of paint. (Duco was a trade name of the industrial paint manufacturer DuPont.)

Krasner described Pollock's painting method thus:

Using sticks and hardened or worn-out brushes (which were in effect like sticks) and basting syringes, he'd begin. His control was amazing. Using a stick was difficult enough, but the basting syringe was like a giant fountain pen. With it he had to control the flow of the paint as well as his gesture.

Pollock's own view of his method, which he described in 1950, was:

New needs new techniques . . . It seems to me that the modern cannot express this age, the airplane, the atom bomb, the radio, in the old forms of the Renaissance or of any other past culture. Each age finds its own techniques . . . Most of the paint I use is a liquid, flowing kind of paint. The brushes I use are used more as sticks rather than brushes – the brush doesn't touch the surface of the canvas, it's just above.

Danger: artists at work

Artists have always been prepared to take risks for the sake of art, sometimes with fatal consequences. Whether pursuing the perfect colour, cutting bits of themselves or exploring the concept of going off in a boat as an artwork/suicide – being lost at sea – like Bas Jan Ader (1942–1975). Some colours are toxic, notably lead white, orpiment and realgar in the past and more recently cadmiums, chromes, zinc and cobalt. Also the solvents/diluents required with some paints may have inadvertently led to undiagnosed health problems in the artists who used them. Little research has been done into the effects of paint on artists, as they are creators who tend not to be much concerned with their own safety and often ignore hazard warnings. I was told of a salesman selling masks that protect against solvent and small particle inhalation who said that it was pretty pointless trying to get artists to wear them; and unless they

Photograph by Harry Shunk of an
'Anthropometric' performance at the International
Gallery of Contemporary Art, Paris, 1960

Yves Klein, *Untitled
Anthropometry*, 1961,
International Klein Blue on
paper mounted on canvas,
1560 × 1080 mm
Musée Cantini, Marseilles

are producing work on an industrial scale, they are unlikely to have fume and dust extraction machinery.

Here are some warning stories.

Dancing over the surface of his canvases, pouring and dripping a mixture of thinned liquid house paints, car enamel and oil paint, Jackson Pollock, a.k.a. 'Jack the dripper', would have been working directly over the work and getting a heavy dose of the volatile solvent used to thin the paints. The industrial house paints chosen for some parts of his paintings would have given off a heavy toxic aroma. This, combined with his heavy drinking and smoking, may have affected his central nervous system, his liver and kidneys, and perhaps goes some way to explain his reputation as unpredictable and bad-tempered. In 1956 his life abruptly ended in a car crash at speed while drunk; he was forty-four.

For a time during his brief life Yves Klein (1928–1962) believed in a blue world. He made work that was blue; he covered canvases with nothing but blue, he covered reproductions of famous classical sculptures with blue, and he wrote to presidents proposing a Blue Revolution. At a 1960 event at the Paris International Gallery of Contemporary Art, he covered naked models with blue and directed them to press their blued bodies on canvas and paper, as if they were human paintbrushes: a creative collaboration to the accompaniment of his one chord symphony. One wonders what the effect of the paint was on the skin of the lovely girls who participated in these performances, which he entitled 'Anthropometrics'. According to one eye-witness they took a lot of cleaning up.

Klein had been seduced by the gorgeousness of dry powdered French ultramarine but was disappointed that it lost its intensity when bound with oil or other media to make paint. He and a colour merchant friend, Eduard Adam, whose family had been serving the Parisian art community for three generations, evolved a synthetic resin/solvent/pigment ratio that satisfied Klein's desire for pigment that stayed attached to a surface without changing its dry appearance.

Klein was immortalized not only in his artworks but also by the patenting of his International Klein Blue; but this probably also contributed to his demise. During the 1950s he made some of his famous blue paintings in a small Paris flat that was never intended to be a studio. According to his wife (interviewed in 1994), he sealed the doors and windows so that other tenants would not smell the fumes of the sovent used to create the paint. In doing so he created a toxic environment that damaged vital organs. He died aged thirty-four after a series of heart attacks – all for sake of a perfect blue.

Both Pollock and Klein were very seduced by paint. Pollock wanted to become paint and make it dance, Klein wanted the world to be a particular colour. Either they were ignorant of the risks they were taking or they didn't care.

Art for all

Today everyone has experience of acrylics in one form or another. Children in nurseries and schools use them. They are so much easier to use and nicer than the kind of materials used in schools before acrylics were made. In the first half of the twentieth century a child in nursery or school would probably have had access to an inferior set of watercolours with an unusable brush or, worse than that, the horrible tins of powder paint used on grey sugar paper. Perhaps nastiest of all were the wax crayons that I remember using when I first started school. Even then I realized they were not doing the job. At least they were non-toxic but there was little joy to be had from their use. The colours were not very strong and their workability bore no relation to artists' paints. Acrylic transformed what schoolchildren could use in the art room.

For amateur artists and professionals acrylics were easier to use than oil paints, less toxic and smelly. Within a couple of generations many artists have switched to them, and some have never used anything else.

Today the range of materials available to artists is enormous. Artists' materials are big business. This is both good and not so good. The good is that everyone has access to materials and can enjoy experiencing them. The bad is that lots of materials are sold and not used because people don't know what to do with them. Good for business but a waste of money for the consumer. If you want to use painting and drawing materials, whether amateur or professional, perhaps a little back-to-basics understanding of what to do with them would be useful. Books and the internet are available to help.

Joseph Beuys (1921–1986) stated that 'everyone is an artist'. His own preferred materials were mud, fat and felt. Whatever the choice of materials, a knowledge and understanding of what they are and how to use them can make the ideas the artist wishes to express into a lasting reality.

Artists' pigments:
A partial description of the artist's palette, ancient and modern

Advances in colour chemistry in the 19th and 20th centuries led to a dramatic increase in the range of colours available. Chemically produced pigments can be manipulated to produce different hues from the same basic element – for example, chrome yellow, green or orange – so there is an infinite number of post 17th century colours; only a few important ones are mentioned here.

A = animal **V** = vegetable **M** = mineral **CH** = chemical
C = pre-17th-century pigment that has not been synthesized and continues in common use in its original form

until the 17th century

post 17th century Significant new colours

BLUES

Ultramarine **M** The most prized of colours, derived from the mineral lapis lazuli, worth more than twice its weight in gold; the best lapis comes from Afghanistan; Cennino has an excellent description of the (lengthy) process of preparing the pigment

Azurite **M** A blue mineral, less valuable than lapis and often used for large areas of sky and sea; it can look a bit green because it is chemically the same as malachite green

Smalt **M** Ground glass coloured with cobalt

Indigo **V** A pigment and dye obtained from various plants, chiefly *Indigofera tinctoria* and woad

Blue verditer **CH** 1600s Similar in hue to azurite
Cobalt **CH** 1803 Inky blue
French ultramarine **CH** 1826 Synthesizes lapis lazuli (from soda, silica, alumina and sulphur) and is much cheaper
Prussian blue **CH** 1710 Used in place of indigo

GREENS

Terre verte **M** Green earth colour often used as underpaint for flesh

Malachite **M** Sister colour of azurite

Verdigris **M** Manufactured by exposing copper to acetic acid fumes

Pansy, lily, sap green **V** Delicate greens used in illuminated manuscripts

Viridian **CH** *c.* 1838–62 Used in place of malachite and verdigris; very bright and translucent
Emerald green **CH** 1814 Used in place of malachite and verdigris; very bright and opaque
Cobalt green **CH** 1780 Transparent, strong hue
Oxide of chromium **CH** *c.*1809 Used in place of terre verte; opaque

until the 17th century

EARTHS, OCHRES AND YELLOWS

All the earth colours have been used since ancient times and continue in use today. Different shades are found all over the world. These are the most readily available pigments, requiring very little preparation — washing, sieving, drying and combining with a binder.

Raw umber **M, C** Grey/brown iron oxide; very useful added to flesh colour mixes and shadows

Burnt umber **M, C** Heated to become a richer, warmer brown

Raw sienna **M, C** Yellowish brown

Burnt sienna **M, C** Heated to become a warmer, redder brown; useful in flesh colour mixtures and sometimes as a red

Yellow and brown ochres **M, C** Variety of shades, mainly opaque

Gold **M** Nuggets beaten until they are gossamer thin become gold leaf; gold paint is made from powdered gold

Orpiment (King's yellow) **M** Poisonous yellow arsenic sulphide, found in desert areas and imported into Europe; this lovely golden yellow is sometimes used as a cheaper substitute for gold

Lead tin yellow **CH** A creamy yellow made from lead tin oxide

Gamboge **V, C** A transparent gum resin

post 17th century Significant new colours

Indian yellow **A** 18th century Said to be derived from the urine of cows that have been fed on mango leaves; powerful transparent hue; good for glazing and better in watercolour than oil

Naples yellow **CH** 18th century Creamy yellow used in place of lead tin yellow

Chrome yellow **CH** 1820s Very bright, used in place of orpiment

Cadmium yellow **CH** 1840s Varying shades but bright, used in place of orpiment.

Zinc yellow **CH** 1850s Bright lemon yellow

ORANGES AND REDS

Realgar **M** Bright orange arsenic sulphide from the same source as orpiment

Vermilion **M, C** From mercuric sulphide, and the brightest red on the early palette; found in volcanic areas but can be manufactured

Carmine **A, C** Purplish red from carminic acid harvested from the female cochineal beetle; used in illuminated manuscripts and for transparent glazes

Lac **A** Red from lac insects, whose bodies are protected by sticky red excretions during their life cycle as they feed on the sap of acacia; from India

Madder **V** Red dye obtained from the roots of the madder plant; as a pigment its natural transparency but rich hue makes it especially useful for glazing over opaque reds and blues

Brasil **V** Dye from the bark of the brasilwood tree; found mainly in medieval illuminated manuscripts

Alizarin crimson **CH, V** 1868 Madder manipulated to be a stronger hue

Cadmium red **CH** 1907 Bright opaque red; used in place of vermilion

Mauve 1856 **CH** The first dyestuff to be produced from coal tar

until the 17th century

BROWNS

Ashphaltum **M** Tar-like substance; transparent brown used for
   glazing and shadows in oil painting
Mummy **A, C** Similar to ashphaltum, but its origin is more sinister –
   though not quite as sinister as it sounds! A gooey tar-like substance
   was used as part of the preserving process for mummies; it was this
   rather than the bodies that was needed for the paint.
Bistre **V** Boiled wood soot for ink and paint
Sepia **A, C** The ink of cuttlefish

BLACKS

Ivory black **A, C** Soot from burnt tusk or horn
Fruit stone black **V, C** Soot from woody fruit stones
Lamp black **V, C** Soot from candle smoke

WHITES

Chalk **M** Not very good white – slightly transparent
Lead white **M, C** Made from lead plates exposed to acetic acid to
   form a white crust; the best white for paint

Zinc white (also known as Chinese white) **CH** 1830s More
   suitable as watercolour

until the 17th century

RED EARTH   CINNABAR   LEAD WHITE   RAW UMBER

YELLOW EARTH   ORPIMENT   RED LEAD   BURNT UMBER

CARBON BLACK   EGYPTIAN BLUE FRIT   MASSICOT   RAW SIENNA

CHALK   INDIGO   VERDIGRIS   BURNT SIENNA

MALACHITE   MADDER   VERMILION   TERRE VERTE

AZURITE   GAMBOGE   LEAD TIN YELLOW

GROUND ULTRAMARINE   GENUINE ULTRAMARINE

post 17th century   Significant new colours

PRUSSIAN BLUE   LEMON YELLOW BARIUM CHROMATE   CADMIUM RED   HANSA/WINDSOR YELLOW   DIOXAZINE VIOLET

NAPLES YELLOW   LEMON YELLOW STRONTIUM CHROMATE   ZINC WHITE   PHTHALOCYANINE BLUE   MARS BLACK

INDIAN YELLOW   ZINC YELLOW   CHINESE WHITE   PHTHALOCYANINE GREEN   LAMP BLACK

COBALT BLUE   OXIDE OF CHROMIUM   COBALT GREEN   ALIZARIN CRIMSON   IVORY BLACK

FRENCH ULTRAMARINE   VIRIDIAN   CERULEAN BLUE   QUINACRIDONE PERMANENT ROSE   MANGANESE BLUE

EMERALD GREEN   CADMIUM YELLOW   AUREOLIN   QUINACRIDONE PERMANENT MAGENTA   TITANIUM WHITE

CHROME YELLOW   MAUVE

153

Further reading

Ames-Lewis, Francis, *Drawing in Early Renaissance Italy*, Yale University Press, New Haven and London, 1981

Arts Council of Great Britain, *Frescoes from Florence*, Arts Council of Great Britain, 1969

Backhouse, Janet, *Books of Hours*, British Library Publishing, London, 1985

Ball, Philip, *Bright Earth, The Invention of Colour*, Vintage Books, London, 2001

Berry, Martyn, Colin Osborne and Anthea Peppin, *The Chemistry of Art*, Royal Society of Chemistry and National Gallery, London, 1999

Bomford, David, Jo Kirby, John Leighton and Ashok Roy, *Art in the Making: Impressionism*, National Gallery Publications, London, 1990

Bomford, David, Jill Dunkerton, Dillian Gordon and Ashok Roy, *Art in the Making: Italian Painting before 1400*, National Gallery Publications, London, 1994

Bower, Peter, *Turner's Papers*, Tate Publications, London, 1990

Brown, J., *Goya's Last Works*, Yale University Press, New Haven and London, 2006

Brown, Michelle P., *Understanding Illuminated Manuscripts*, British Library Publishing, London, 1994

Callan, Anthea, *Techniques of the Impressionists*, Chartwell Books, 1982

Cennini, Cennino d'Andrea, *The Craftsman's Handbook: Il Libro dell'Arte*, Dover Publications, New York, 1954

Coombes, Katherine, *The Portrait Miniature in England*, Victoria and Albert Museum Publications, London, 1998

Chapman, Hugo, *Michelangelo Drawings: Closer to the Master*, British Museum Publications, London, 2005

De Hamel, Christopher, *Scribes and Illuminators*, British Museum Publications, London, 1992

— *The British Library Guide to Manuscript Illumination*, British Library Publishing, London, 2001

Dunkerton, Jill, Susan Foister and Nicholas Penny, *Durer to Veronese, Sixteenth-Century Painting in the National Gallery*, National Gallery Publications, London, 1999

Dunkerton, Jill, Susan Foister, Dillian Gordon and Nicholas Penny *Giotto to Durer, Early Renaissance Painting in the National Gallery*, Yale University Press, New Haven and London, 1991

Enzo, Carli d', I Grandi Maestri del Trecento Toscano, Istituto Italiano D'Arte Grafiche, Bergamo, 1961

Edmond, Mary, *Hilliard and Oliver: Lives and Works of Two Great Miniaturists*, Robert Hale, 1983

Foister, Susan, Ashok Roy and Martin Wyld, *Holbein's Ambassadors*, Yale University Press, New Haven and London, 2008

Garfield, Simon, *Mauve: How One Man Invented a Colour that Changed the World*, Faber and Faber, London, 2000

Gettens, Rutherford J., and George L. Stout, *Painting Materials: A Short Encyclopedia*, Dover Publications, New York, 1942

Hackney, Stephen (editor), *Completing the Picture*, Tate Publishing, London, 1982

Hall, Marcia B., and Takashi Okamura, *Michelangelo: Frescoes of the Sistine Chapel*, Harry N. Abrams, Inc., New York, 2002

Hamilton, James, *Turner and the Scientists*, Tate Publications, London, 1998

Harley, Rosamund D., *Artists' Pigments 1600–1835*, Butterworth, London, 1970

Hebborn, Eric, *The Art Forger's Handbook*, Cassell, London, 1997

Herbert, R.L., *Seurat and the Making of La Grande Jatte*, Art Institute of Chicago, 2004

Hilliard, Nicholas, *The Art of Limning*, Carcanet Press, Manchester, 1981

Hirst, Michael, *Michelangelo and His Drawings*, Yale University Press, New Haven and London, 1988

Hockney, David, *Hockney on Hockney*, Thames and Hudson, London, 1976

International Institute of Conservation, *Dublin Conference Papers*, 1998

—— *Studies in Conservation*, vol. 43, 1998

Johnston, Edward, *Writing and Illuminating and Lettering*, A. and C. Black, London, 1906

King, Ross, *Michelangelo and the Pope's Ceiling*, Pimlico, London, 2006

Kren, Thomas, and Mark Evans (ed.), *A Masterpiece Reconstructed: The Hours of Louis XII*,
    Getty Publications, Los Angeles, 2006

Letheve, Jacques, *The Daily Life of French Artists in the Nineteenth Century*, Allen and Unwin,
    London, 1968

Lucie-Smith, Edward, *The Faber Book of Art Anecdotes*, Faber and Faber, London, 1992

MacGregor, Neil, *Making Masterpieces*, BBC Publications, London, 1997

Mayer, Ralph, *Dictionary of Art Terms and Techniques*, A. and C. Black, London, 1969

——*The Artist's Handbook of Materials and Techniques*, Faber and Faber, London, 1991

National Gallery, *Technical Bulletin*, vol. 27, National Gallery Publications, London, 2006

Norgate, Edward, *Miniatura or the Art of Limning*, Yale University Press, New Haven and London, 1997

Phoenix Art Museum, *Copper as Canvas: Two Centuries of Masterpiece Paintings on Copper,*
    1575–1775, Phoenix Art Museum, Phoenix, Arizona, 1998

Spurling, Hilary, *The Unknown Matisse*, Penguin, London, 1998

—— *Matisse the Master*, Hamish Hamilton, London, 2005

Strong, Roy, and V. J. Murrell, *Artists of the Tudor Court: The Portrait Miniature Rediscovered,*
    1520–1620, Victoria and Albert Museum Publications, London, 1983

Thompson, Daniel V., *The Materials and Techniques of Medieval Painting*, Yale University Press,
    New Haven and London, 1936

—— *The Practice of Tempera Painting*, Dover Publications, New York, 1936

Townsend, Joyce H., *Turner's Painting Techniques*, Tate Publications, London, 2005

Vasari, Giorgio, *The Lives of the Artists*, Oxford Paperbacks, 1991

——*Vasari on Technique*, Dover Publications, New York, 1960

Watrous, James, *The Craft of Old Master Drawings*, University of Wisconsin Press, 2006

Wettering, Ernst van de, *Rembrandt, The Painter at Work*, Amsterdam University Press, 2000

Whitly, Kathleen, *The Gilded Page: The History and Technique of Manuscript Gilding,*
    British Library Publishing, London, 2000

Wilcox, Timothy, *The Triumph of Watercolours*, Philip Wilson, London, 2005

Index

Page numbers in *italic* refer to illustrations and captions

Acknowledgements

Author's acknowledgements

I wish to thank, first, all the museums, galleries and libraries where I have spent many happy hours discovering wonderful things that artists have made.

I greatly appreciate the help I have received from my colleagues in the Education Department of Dulwich Picture Gallery, and from the Manuscripts Department at the British Library, Alan Derbyshire and Timea Tallian at the Victoria and Albert Museum, and Tim Noad and Anne Ginige at the College of Arms.

Thanks are due to the staff at A.P. Fitzpatrick for materials and information over the years, and to the staff at Winsor and Newton brushmaking factory in Lowestoft.

Particular thanks must go to Patricia Monahan for encouraging me to approach publishers with the idea for this book; to John Nicoll at Frances Lincoln for taking me on; to my editor, Jo Christian, whose encouragement and enthusiasm kept me going through the making of the book; to Becky Clarke for her sensitive and thoughtful design; to Sue Gladstone for all her help in researching the illustrations; and to Richard Cork for the foreword. I wish also to thank Hilary Lane, Janet Locke and Susan Wadbrook.

I must acknowledge the influence of the late Stephen Rees Jones of the Courtauld Insitute, who was a patient, kind and inspirational teacher.

And, finally, thanks to Sophie, Jonathan and Michael, who helped in so many ways.